MMB

MMB MUSIC, INC.

CONTEMPORARY ARTS BUILDING
3526 WASHINGTON AVENUE
SAINT LOUIS, MISSOURI 63103-1019 USA
314 531-9635; 800 543-3771 (USA/Canada); Fax 314 531-8384
http://www.mmbmusic.com

Adolescent
Art
Therapy

by

Debra Greenspoon Linesch

BRUNNER/MAZEL, *Publishers* • NEW YORK
A member of the Taylor & Francis Group

Library of Congress Cataloging-in-Publication Data

Linesch, Debra Greenspoon,
  Adolescent art therapy.

  Bibliography: p. 241
  Includes index.
  1. Art therapy for youth. I. Title. [DNLM:
1. Art therapy—in adolescence. WS 463 L754a]
RJ505.A7L56 1988   616.89′1656   87–21866
ISBN 0–87630–486–2

Copyright © 1988 by Debra Greenspoon Linesch

For information and ordering, contact:
Brunner/Mazel
A member of the Taylor & Francis Group
47 Runway Road, Suite G
Levittown, PA 19057-4700
1-800-821-8312

MANUFACTURED IN THE UNITED STATES OF AMERICA

10 9 8 7 6

Foreword

Effective therapists, regardless of their psychological orientation, must have the ability to speak the language of their patients' inner world if they are to promote movement or growth within their patients' psychic structures. Furthermore, the therapists and the shared language they create with their patients must possess a subtlety and a range of depth and pace so that their patients can handle and integrate new psychic material. Otherwise, therapists are likely to find themselves overwhelming or underwhelming their patients, and they are as likely to foster fear as understanding or positive change.

This challenge of finding a mutually comprehensible and suitable language for therapy is particularly critical when working with adolescents. Words and formal language may not be fully developed in an adolescent, or heavy reliance on the part of the therapist just on words can turn off an adolescent since the very notion of words is so strongly associated with the adult/straight/authority world. Symbolic play, on the other side, which is often effective with children, is likely to be rejected by adolescents as too regressive and hence threatening. Also, the play therapy process may lack the necessary subtlety to express the increasingly complex world of the adolescent.

The use of visual means to express affect and psychological states has several powerful attributes that lend themselves effectively to the therapy process. Visual images, creations, and metaphors can fill the gap between play therapy and straight verbal therapy. As a consequence, this melding of a shared visual communication system and the therapeutic process, in what is now called "art therapy," has considerable potential when doing therapeutic work in general, and quite specifically with adolescents.

Any therapist who does dream analysis will know how certain images for a patient will crystalize entire months of therapy work or how the dream image can lead to a sudden clarification of a conflict. Just as potent are experiences that patients report of how a visual image from their childhood or even from a recent interpersonal encounter can provide them with a profound understanding of what has been happening to them psychologically; such an image can encapsulate "everything at once" or telescope years of experience into a graspable pattern.

Shaman and medicine men from ancient traditions have long known the power of an image to infuse or release psychic energy. Even in the more conventional approaches to medical healing, visualization is beginning to be recognized as a way to alter one's whole attitude about a situation. The reason that a picture can be worth a thousand words may be based on the neurophysiological and psychological fact that the brain's cerebral hemispheres have different means of processing information. Currently, the thinking is that the right hemisphere works like an image: wholistic or gestalt-like, whereby it takes in large amounts of information, even logically contradictory information, simultaneously, and holds it all together or displays it as a mental image. This is in contrast to the left hemisphere which takes in and processes information in a sequential, linear fashion, much like the words on this page, using a logic filter to determine what is real or what fits. Because so much of the material that is crucial to change in therapy is concerned with coexisting contradictions and conflicts, the right hemisphere and its wholistic imagery comes much closer to capturing this experience than does the left hemisphere with its linear approach. Thus, a visual image can contain the experience of "I love my mother/I hate my mother" or "I am afraid to go to this new school/I am excited to go to this new school," while the logical word sequence would have difficulty containing these contradictory feelings.

Very possibly because affect is experienced and organized by the infant long before verbal language and linear experience is known, and/ or because affective states by their nature are omnipresent and filled with contradictions, a visual image is more likely than words to closely parallel the language of emotions.

Adolescent Art Therapy demonstrates the effectiveness and power of using visual images with adolescent patients as they struggle to represent, defend, heal, comprehend, and integrate their unconscious or partly conscious world. For those therapists who have come to depend heavily on sequential verbal language (myself being one), Ms. Linesch has skillfully synthesized the sequential process that underlies art therapy, while richly documenting and illustrating her wholistic understanding of the therapy process with the actual visual productions of the patients she discusses. In many ways, this book represents the best of both worlds, or one might say, the best of both hemispheres. Ordinarily, the therapeutic process is synergistically strengthened, as the value in this book is, when images and words are brought together. Ms. Linesch's verbal analysis sets the stage for the visual work of her patients, and by doing so, she puts these images in context and lays out in a stepwise fashion what is taking place psychologically behind the "scenes." Like a well-prepared case study, this book provides the reader with a longitudinal understanding of the linear steps in a psychological development, while simultaneously presenting a visual cross-sectional picture of what is taking place at any particular moment. By using many clinical examples, Ms. Linesch demonstrates how she and the adolescent through the sensitive choice of art materials and directives can regulate the degree of self-disclosure, affect intensity, and psychological distance whether in individual, group, or family sessions. Ms. Linesch further delineates the way that later titling and retrospective viewing of the art productions allows for selective reinforcing, amplifying, and clarifying key psychological points while using the artwork to maintain a stable and safe therapeutic framework.

Thus, in a number of ways, this book explains how art therapy can serve as a universal language for the therapeutic process, and one that can be embraced by adolescents without having to surrender their limited but hard-won emerging individuation.

David S. May, M.D.
Assistant Clinical Professor of Psychiatry,
UCLA Medical Center

Contents

Introduction

Adolescent Art Therapy is an attempt to delineate the issues and techniques that are particular to the practice of art psychotherapy with an adolescent population. Adolescence is a stage of development with unique difficulties that make psychotherapy very complex. Many of the struggles experienced by the adolescent involve conflicts of identity and self-expression. These conflicts can be made accessible for exploration through art productions in a way that they cannot through verbal expression. The youngster's developmentally appropriate defenses tend to block insight-oriented verbal psychotherapy. Art therapy can help the adolescent master and utilize the very struggles that prevent him/her from participation in traditional psychotherapy.

Adolescent Art Therapy provides a developmentally oriented rationale for the use of art psychotherapy with the adolescent patient. To do this, it examines the developmental stage of adolescence and correlates the psychotherapeutic needs of the adolescent with the psychotherapeutic potential in the art therapy modality. In addition, it outlines and explores the different kinds of settings and the different kinds of approaches that can be used with adolescents. It provides an overview of art therapy techniques with severely disturbed, delinquent and highly functioning youngsters by exploring art therapy practice in hospitals, residential treatment centers and outpatient clinics. It addresses the use of art therapy with adolescents in family and group treatment and it introduces current research with adolescents that further validates the use of art therapy. Overall, it provides a comprehensive look at the modality of art therapy with the adolescent population.

The first chapter provides an overview of adolescence and examines the relationships between the specific issues of this developmental stage and the concept of creativity. This framework is then used to explore the case material that comprises a large portion of this book.

The second chapter introduces the art psychotherapy modality, focusing on how the adolescent's artwork can be used for assessment. The kinds of psychopathology manifested in adolescence are described and the interplay between emotional disorders and self-expression is discussed. Each relevant diagnostic category of the *Diagnostic and Statistical Manual of Mental Disorders, Third Edition–Revised (DSM-III-R)* is illustrated with artwork done by disturbed youngsters. The psychopathology is explored as it manifests itself symptomatically in the art pieces.

The third chapter is an overview of art therapy approaches in work with the adolescent population. The nature of the therapeutic relationship, the flexible use of art therapy directives and the importance of media selection in the treatment of adolescents are considered.

The fourth chapter compares and contrasts two different approaches by presenting two case studies that demonstrate the treatment modality of art psychotherapy with adolescent patients. The two case examples represent very different psychopathologies. The first case presents the use of art psychotherapy with a conduct-disordered adolescent and illustrates techniques utilized with youngsters who are capable of insight orientation. The second case presents the use of art psychotherapy with a severely disturbed adolescent and illustrates techniques utilized with youngsters exhibiting psychotic tendencies and placed in inpatient facilities.

The fifth chapter discusses how the art therapy modality can be utilized in institutions that rely on the treatment team approach. It explores the concept of "adjunctive" art therapy and attempts to provide a model for the integration of art psychotherapy within a psychodynamic approach to treatment.

The sixth chapter provides a theoretical framework for the use of group art therapy with adolescents. Case material is used to illustrate a variety of group-dynamic issues in discussing the details of a long-term art therapy group with four adolescent girls.

The seventh chapter is an overview of the kinds of interventions that can be used with an adolescent in conjunction with family members. Case material examined includes art therapy projects done by dyads, triads and larger family groups involving siblings and parents.

The final chapter presents an example of art therapy research with an adolescent population. A clinical study that analyzes the artwork of 12 youngsters placed in a therapeutic school demonstrates the relationship between self-expression and participation in milieu treatment.

The author gratefully acknowledges permission to use the case examples and illustrations appearing in this book. They have all been disguised to provide complete anonymity.

Adolescent Art Therapy fills an empty niche in the literature. Adolescence is unique developmentally and the art therapy approach to this age range merits the kind of intensive examination that this book provides.

1

Adolescence and
the Creative Process

One of the underlying themes of this book is a belief in the particularly powerful relationship between emotional health and self-expression in adolescence. It is the intent of this chapter to explore and present clinical information that supports that relationship. Although a large portion of *Adolescent Art Therapy* presents case material in an effort to demonstrate the art therapy modality, that material is of little value without this theoretical framework.

To introduce the most important literature, which forms the bulk of the clinical material on adolescence, several authors are examined and the traditional psychoanalytic views on adolescence and creativity are summarized. This review will provide the groundwork for the less traditional concepts to be delineated in the final sections of this chapter. Following the examination of the theoretical material, the principles of psychodynamically oriented art therapy with adolescents, which represent innovative departures from traditional clinical practice, are examined in relation to the literature. Despite the fact that many clinicians have recognized the potency of creativity in the emotional life of the adolescent, none but the art therapists have attempted to base their treatment on this understanding. The analyses of case material, which comprise a large part of *Adolescent Art Therapy,* provide a clinical rationalization for such an approach to treatment.

The brief review of the literature begins with an effort to define adolescence. Most obviously, adolescence is the stage of development that immediately follows the latency stage and begins with the physical event of puberty. Generally the physical changes of puberty begin around the age of twelve and catapult the previously "settled" child into a turbulent six to eight year process. However, it is important to understand the adolescent experience as much more than a set of physical reactions. To a great extent, adolescence is the psychic response to these physical changes. Blos (1962) most cogently describes the intrapsychic efforts of the adolescent to adjust to puberty with the internal ego apparatus developed during the latency stage:

> Adolescence is here viewed as the sum total of all attempts at adjustment to the stage of puberty, to the new set of inner and outer—endogenous and exogenous—conditions which confront the individual. The urgent necessity to cope with the novel condition of puberty evokes all the modes of excitation, tension, gratification and defense that ever played a role in previous years—that is, during the psychosexual development of infancy and early childhood. (p. 11)

Psychoanalytic theory goes on to explain how the resolution of the intrapsychic struggles differs significantly from the resolution accomplished at the end of early childhood. At this time of the second individuation, the adolescent must separate from the family and create an independent identity. Unlike the identification process which allowed the younger child to remain closely tied to parental figures while resolving his/her psychosexual conflicts, the adolescent is faced with separation from the family and, consequently, a lack of self-definition. Erikson (1950) clearly describes the task of the adolescent as the creation of an identity in counteraction to the potential for role confusion:

> The growing and developing youths, faced with this physio-logical revolution within them, and with tangible adult tasks

4

ahead of them are now primarily concerned with what they appear to be in the eyes of others as compared with what they feel they are, and with the question of how to connect the roles and skills cultivated earlier with the occupational prototypes of the day. (p. 261)

The adolescent is faced with an enormous task, one that can be accomplished only with the experimentation and rebelliousness that have come to be typical of teenage youngsters in our society. When the difficult process of self-definition is understood, the adolescent's testing of self and of others can be seen as productive and useful. However, it is crucial that the latency stage will have furnished the youngster with the tools to accomplish the tasks of adolescence. Without the control of ego functions developed before puberty, the adolescent will have difficulty surviving the turbulent reorganization required of his/her emotional life.

It is the search for heterosexual object relations outside the family that propels adolescents through their struggles to adapt to the vicissitudes of their libidos. Many adolescents experience themselves as if in a void at this time. Emotionally and profoundly separated from their families, as yet having found no substitutional attachment, and confused about their sexual feelings, adolescents typically feel self-absorbed and isolated. It is these feelings that contribute to the adolescent propensity toward creativity, one of the very important points to be made in this chapter. Blos (1962) repeatedly points out the importance of fantasy life and creativity as a way for the alienated adolescent to communicate personal experiences. For some youngsters, creative expression provides the only vehicle for social participation. Blos says:

> The heightened introspection or psychological closeness to internal processes in conjunction with a distance from outer objects allow the adolescent a freedom of experience and an access to his feelings which promote a state of delicate sensitivity and perceptiveness. Adolescent artistic productions are often undisguisedly autobiographical and reach their height during phases of libidinal withdrawal from the object world . . . The creative productivity thus represents an effort to accomplish urgent tasks of internal transformations. (p. 125)

Malmquist (1978) agrees with Blos's evaluation of the role of creativity in the adolescent's accomplishment of developmental tasks. In

Handbook of Adolescence he points out the potential for misunderstanding the typical developmental conflicts of adolescence as signs of illness. He goes on to explain the clinical value of understanding the adolescent's cryptic signals as efforts to master intrapsychic struggles. In doing so he points out the value of fantasy (and creativity) as one of the essential requirements for continued ego strength during adolescence:

> Fantasy is required to aid in the delay of gratification when interferences from reality conflict with what is desired and can also be used for creative, academic or vocational pursuits. Without fantasy, enjoyment of the arts is impossible beyond a purely sensory level. (p. 47)

It is clear that creativity and self-expression, which provide outlets for fantasy, are important aids in the difficult tasks facing the adolescent. The healthy youngster, equipped with the gains in ego strength from the long learning period of latency, generally exhibits a resurgence of expressive zeal. As Blos (1962) points out, teenage diaries and journals are good examples of this process. The healthy youngster is able to find ways of exploring and experimenting with identity concerns by harnessing the creativity that will help his/her transition from child to adult. Not so fortunate is the adolescent whose development is impeded by early family and environmental difficulties that leave him/her lacking the tools for spontaneous creative expression.

With this understanding, the value of psychotherapy based on creative expression seems natural for the adolescent stage of development. When creativity is understood as a requisite for emotional maturation, it can be appreciated as a potentially healing force for development that has been delayed or distorted. It is the field of art therapy that develops this fundamental principle of the psychodynamic theory of adolescence into a treatment technique. Landgarten (1981) represents the field of psychodynamically oriented art therapy when she says:

> Both the preconditions essential to adolescent character formation and the developmental tasks of adolescence may be worked upon through the art psychotherapy modality. (p. 156)

This simple statement is full of implications for the treatment of adolescents. At a stage of development when conflicts, turmoil and change are all paramount, it is counterproductive to conceptualize treatment independent of the needs of the evolving ego. Since the adolescent ego depends on self-expression and creativity, it is imperative to include these concepts in treatment considerations. Art therapy which bases corrective emotional experiences in art expression may, in fact, be a modality of choice for this difficult age group.

The remainder of *Adolescent Art Therapy* illustrates the ways in which art expression can facilitate therapeutic progress. Throughout all the case material presented, the underlying principle remains the same: art expression, as a developmentally appropriate modality, provides the adolescent with an ego-syntonic aid in his/her difficult struggles.

Before beginning to explore the case material, it is important to investigate the manner in which psychopathology can manifest itself in the art expression of the disturbed adolescent. This investigation provides the reader with an introduction into ways in which art productions can communicate the intrapsychic dynamics of the adolescent whose behavior may make little or no sense to the observing clinician. Chapter 2 thus links the theoretical formulations discussed here with the case examples that follow.

2

Diagnosis and
Art Expression

In this chapter types of adolescent psychopathology are related to symptomatic manifestations in art expression through discussion of specific categories of assessment. Concrete evidence that the artistic expression of adolescents does correspond with their intrapsychic life is seen within the art productions. This chapter thus paves the way for the remaining sections of this book which look at specific case material by developing a starting point for the appreciation of the role of artistic expression in the treatment of adolescent psychopathology.

For the most part, the diagnostic categories outlined for adolescence in the *Diagnostic and Statistical Manual of Mental Disorders (DSM-III-R)* are followed. Since the *DSM-III-R* differentiates the diagnoses from a behavioral, descriptive perspective, however, it has limited (organizational) value for the purposes of this chapter. In order to retain its clarity but avoid its oversimplification, the *DSM-III-R* is used as a framework and the diagnostic discussions are supplemented by the more psychodynamic orientation found in Malmquist's (1978) *Handbook of Adolescence*. Despite the danger of potentially limiting the framework developed in this chapter, a single-author supplementation to the *DSM-III-R* descriptions is used to retain consistency.

Before looking at the specific categories of adolescent psychopathology, the defense mechanisms most typical of this developmental stage are examined. The decision to preface the investigation of adolescent disorders with a scrutiny of adaptive and maladaptive defense mechanisms reflects the underlying orientation of this volume. When adolescence is understood as the struggle of the ego to function autonomously and develop an adaptive identity, the disorders of this stage can be understood as defensive overreactions to the ego's failures. An understanding of the defenses most commonly seen in teenage youngsters will enrich the subsequent discussion of the complex categories of psychopathology.

Examples of art productions are included to depict most of the defense mechanisms and the diagnostic categories discussed. These examples illustrate how art expression can both display the symptomatic manifestations of each disorder and, at the same time, suggest the unconscious conflicts that are behind the manifest problems, thereby integrating the behavioral approach *(DSM-III-R)* with the psychodynamic (Malmquist).

THE DEFENSE MECHANISMS

The defense mechanisms characteristic of adolescence fulfill two functions, either responding to the anxiety generated by separation efforts with parental figures or reacting to the impulses that are consequent to unsuccessful attempts to separate. Malmquist (1978) lists four defense mechanisms that adolescents typically employ in their struggles against the old attachments of childhood. To facilitate their emancipation from latency-stage object ties, the adolescent utilizes defensive maneuvers as he/she strives for autonomy. These efforts, best understood as adaptive, infuse this stage with its characteristic quality of alienation. Malmquist lists *displacement, reversal of affect, narcissism* and *regression* as the four predominant defenses of this type (p. 55).

Malmquist describes five other defenses that the adolescent employs when he/she is unable to successfully utilize these intrapsychic maneuvers to separate from the early attachments. When the defenses against attachment fail, the adolescent experiences the surfacing of intolerable impulses and is compelled to utilize different, generally less adaptive defensive strategies. Malmquist lists *repression and denial, asceticism, intellectualization, noncompromise* and *isolation* in this category (p. 57).

Artwork has been selected to demonstrate these defense mechanisms. In all of the examples it is possible to recognize the defensive style of the adolescent artist. Although in many cases more than one defense mechanism is operative and obvious at the same time, the illustrations portray the manner in which adolescents develop characteristic defensive attitudes. Consequently, the examples chosen illustrate the predominant defense despite the possible presence of additional mechanisms.

Displacement

The defense mechanism of displacement is operative when the adolescent seeks attachments (often exaggerated) outside of the family to avoid anxiety-ridden relationships with old object ties. This mechanism is an adaptive one, allowing the adolescent to form transitional attachments that aid in the separation process and help the youngster through the difficult period before genuine heterosexual relationships can be created. Displacement must be understood before the function of other, less adaptive mechanisms can be appreciated. No artwork has been selected to illustrate this defense mechanism since it is typically manifest in an adaptive (i.e., nonclinical) population.

Reversal of Affect

This complicated defense mechanism operates when the adolescent is less able to separate from early object relationships and instead of displacing the relationships, he/she replaces the attachment with hostility. With this defense, the adolescent remains tightly connected to the family members and consequently riddled with ambivalence.

The collage in Figure 1, done by a fifteen-year-old boy in response to a directive encouraging him to portray his relationship with his father, illustrates this defense mechanism clearly. The youngster represented himself on the left side of the paper, a tight-lipped expression of anger that he described as "always ready to blow." He depicted his father,

11

Figure 1

on the right side of the page, as an inflexible statue which he described as "rigid and unmoving." In this powerful art production, the boy laid out a complex intrapsychic dynamic whereby two defense mechanisms combined to create the reversal of affect. Unable to tolerate the anxiety-provoking attachment to his father and struggling with ambivalence regarding separation from his parents (early object relations), this boy reacts by resisting the past attachment *(denial)* and substituting hostility *(reaction formation)*. Unfortunately, this defensive maneuver leaves the youngster tightly bonded; the negative affect has replaced the positive, but effective separation is impossible. A collage such as Figure 1, so concrete a representation of a complicated intrapsychic phenomenon, can be useful in helping an adolescent understand his/her complex feelings. In this case, the collage was subsequently used to focus a discussion on the way that the artist's relationship with his father was connected to his passive-aggressive behavior. It is interesting in this collage to observe the similarity between the "father's" expression and the "self" expression. For this adolescent, the latency stage had been characterized by a strong identification with his father and adolescence became a difficult struggle to understand and loosen those bonds. His artwork, of which Figure 1 is only one example, offered a tremendous aid in understanding the unconscious process that was causing distressing manifest behavior.

Figure 2 was created by a fourteen-year-old boy in response to the therapist's question about his relationship with his parents. He began the complicated drawing with the stick figure self-representation at the top center of the page, describing himself as determined to "get my parents off my back." Apparently contradicting the adamant request to be left alone (represented by the stop sign), the youngster then scribbled a series of chaotic paths leading to his self-representation. After completing the scribble, he confided that "there may be ways to reach me but my parents (drawn, crossed out and then separated from the main section of the drawing) will never find me." The drawing clearly depicts this youth's defensive reaction to the anxiety caused by threatening emotional entanglements with the parental figures. Although the boy attempts to defend against the psychic distress, his attempts to deny the attachment and replace it with a reversal of affect are complicated and leave him with the ambivalence so poignantly displayed in this drawing. He tries valiantly to separate ("stop or else," he says) but provides a path (however inaccessible), undercutting his efforts.

13

Figure 2

Increase in Narcissism

Essentially, this defense mechanism involves aggrandizing the attachment to one's self as a way of avoiding and replacing the distressing and anxiety-provoking attachment to early object relations. Like the defense mechanism of reversal of affect, increase in narcissism helps the adolescent minimize the attachment to early object relations, but in this case redirect the affect toward the self.

Figure 3 is an example of this mechanism in operation. In this drawing, done by a sixteen-year-old girl, in response to the therapist's request to draw her family, the *increase in narcissism* is obvious. The girl drew her family sitting in the bleachers at a baseball game. Although no one seems to be having a good time, and there appears to be little connection between the family members, the girl's self-representation on the right side of the drawing is of central concern. Dad, mom and the two sisters are drawn facing forward, open and available in differing degrees, but all resembling each other in drawing style and posture. The artist's self-representation is strikingly separate, drawn with heavier outlining, more anxiously scratched lines and in a self-absorbed, regressive posture. The drawing suggests the girl's retreat from her family (early object relations) with an affective focus back into herself. Rather than dealing with the anxiety-provoking familial relationships, this adolescent, although physically still a part of the tight family system, defends against the preadolescent bonds with the typically adolescent maneuver of increasing narcissistic involvement.

Regression

Regression can be understood as the adolescent's escape from dealing with separation. With certain adolescents, autonomy may be even more anxiety provoking than the early object relations have become. In such cases the adolescent can employ this defense (regression) and simply alleviate separation anxiety by remaining attached to his/her parents.

Figure 4, a collage created by a fourteen-year-old girl, depicts this regressive maneuver. This collage was created in response to the therapist's suggestion to divide the page into two sections, illustrating one with images that represent herself and the other with images that

Figure 3

Figure 4

represent her mother. The directive was conceived to provide structure for the difficult task of addressing issues of separation. Interestingly, this adolescent divided the page unequally, depicting her mother as adventuresome and self-absorbed all over the majority of the page. In the small section she saved for her own representation, the youngster expressed her regressive cravings. Rather than depict herself as an autonomous adolescent, an identity that would cause too much anxiety and would require affective acknowledgment of mother's emotional abandonment, she portrayed herself in a childlike relationship to a nuclear family. As a clear portrayal of this girl's efforts to avoid any recognition or experience of separation, this collage acted as a clue to her defensive style. As treatment progressed the same collage was later used to help the girl understand her fears and anxieties.

Repression and Denial

These two defenses represent the adolescent's first responses to the impulses that arise because the earlier defensive attempts against attachments (and therefore toward emancipation) were unsuccessful. Efforts to deny and repress these impulses generally take a great toll on the adolescent, requiring large amounts of energy that otherwise could be channeled into activities and relationships.

Figure 5, a marker drawing created by a fifteen-year-old girl, clearly depicts the manner in which many adolescents repress or deny the impulses that arise consequent to their failed attempts at emotional emancipation. The drawing was produced in response to the therapist's request to depict the girl's feelings toward her parents about which she was verbally expressing confusion. The drawing originally was without the associated words, "Locked Feelings," which later became the title. As the artist examined the first part of her drawing (the head in the center of the page), she commented on the clenched teeth "barely able to stop the guck from spilling out," the war paint and the patch slightly askew over one eye. When asked what it was that lay behind these symbolic efforts to "hold things in," the adolescent spontaneously wrote the title and drew the images on the right side of the paper. From this drawing it became clear, to both the adolescent and the therapist, that troubling feelings lay behind the strong denial system.

In addition to laying out the defense mechanism, this drawing concretely pointed out the way to therapeutic progress, providing the symbolic "key" for the unlocking process. Just as the artwork helped

18

LoCKED FeeLiNGS

Figure 5

this adolescent recognize the way in which she defended against the anxiety-provoking impulses, it also helped provide structured imagery to begin the difficult task of examining the material behind the defenses.

Asceticism

With this defense the adolescent continues to struggle against the impulses that arise because of his/her inability to defend against the early attachments. As a way of negating the impulses, the ascetic adolescent permits himself/herself no gratification. No artwork has been selected to illustrate this defense mechanism.

Intellectualization

This defensive maneuver is essentially an overemphasis on cognitive functioning as an attempt to avoid affect. This process allows the adolescent who is struggling with anxiety-provoking impulses to feel that his/her intellect is in control. In this way the adolescent utilizing this defense can cope with the otherwise threatening experience of aggressive or sexual impulses.

Figure 6, a marker drawing created by a fourteen-year-old girl, illustrates this defense mechanism clearly. This drawing was produced spontaneously, without direction, as the girl told the therapist about her relationship with her parents. The winged heart was drawn first, subsequently embellished with the words "I love you." When the therapist puzzled aloud about the heart with wings, the adolescent added the definitions to the right of her original words. Apparently agitated about the ambivalent feelings depicted in the imagery, she utilized the defense mechanism of intellectualization as a way of coping with potentially distressing affect. Rather than explore the meaning of her drawing, she chose to analyze and define the title (focusing on her cognitive abilities), displaying the manner in which she defends against the impulses which are consequent to her inability to separate from the early object relations.

Noncompromise

Rigid adherence to moral, ethical positions is one example of this defense, which operates when adolescents perceive their parents as

20

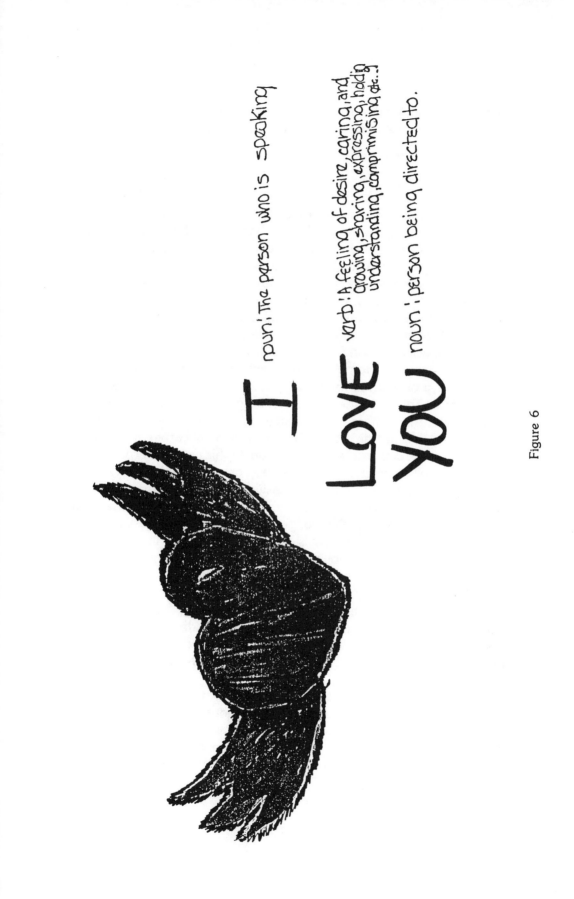

I

noun: The person who is speaking

Love

verb: A feeling of desire, caring, and growing, sharing, expressing, holding, understanding, compromising, etc...)

You

noun: person being directed to.

Figure 6

involved in behavior that is too close to the impulses that threaten them. No artwork has been selected to illustrate this defense.

Isolation

This defense mechanism involves the separation of affect from content. In some cases the affect is repressed, in others it is displaced to another situation. Two examples will help clarify this complex defense.

Figure 7, a marker drawing produced by a fifteen-year-old boy, and Figure 8, a marker drawing produced by a fourteen-year-old boy, illustrate the defensive use of isolation. Both pictures include a heavily accentuated sun, often interpreted as a symbol of the paternal figure. In both cases, as the symbolism suggests, the unavailability of the father complicated the separation process from the intensely attached mother. In Figure 7, a free, undirected drawing, the artist described the farmer as "getting away from home." "Home" is portrayed as a fenced-in, distant entity, not quite as prominent in the drawing as the sun, which is hiding behind dark glasses. This boy's defensive response to the difficult impulses he feels toward his mother, exacerbated by the absence of his father, characterizes his artistic production. Figure 8, a barren and isolated-looking drawing, depicts a similar situation. In this case, the artist included no directly self-representative figure, but provided verbal clues to the intrapsychic material behind the defensive quality of the drawing. Asked about the imagery, he described the mailbox on the right side of the page as "full of mail waiting to get picked up by the postal carrier." The symbolism suggests the boy's ambivalent desire for intimacy despite his defensive efforts. Although the affective quality of this drawing predominantly displays the kind of isolation that this boy utilizes to defend against the feelings aroused in him by his family situation, the picture also provides concrete opportunities, through the symbolic content, for further exploration. Isolated and defended (notice the rigid drawing style and the inaccessibility of the mailbox), the artist uses the metaphor in the art production (mail) to express his desire to be heard and understood.

This exploration of nine defense mechanisms provides an introduction to the discussion of adolescent psychopathology. The following sections of this chapter, which illustrate the variety of adolescent diagnostic categories, refer back to the discussion of defense mechanisms frequently. In all of the artwork to follow, the content and process are

Figure 7

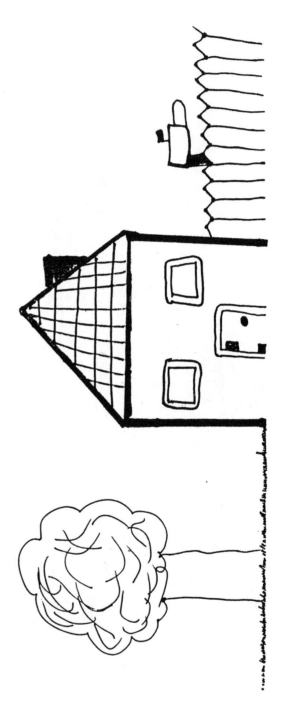

Figure 8

analyzed in terms of the manner in which they illustrate the maladaptive and defensive functioning of the ego in response to developmental or environmental stresses.

DIAGNOSTIC CATEGORIES

A combination of *DSM-III-R* and Malmquist (1978) provides a framework for exploring several of the diagnostic categories of adolescence. The disorders are investigated on two levels: first, in terms of how adolescents' (behavioral) symptomatic manifestations are displayed in their art productions; and second, in terms of how the latent (unconscious) dynamics responsible for the symptoms also become evident in the creative expressions. It is important to note that the *DSM-III-R*'s diagnostic categories are descriptive only, and may include a variety of etiological causes. The artwork was selected to show how the intrapsychic reasons for the behavior (as varied as they may be) can be communicated in the graphic imagery. This approach is not intended to provide or illustrate definitive explanations for the disorders.

DISRUPTIVE BEHAVIOR DISORDERS

Conduct Disorders

In this category the *DSM-III-R* categorizes a group of emotional disorders around their common characteristic of a primarily acting-out manifestation: behavioral criteria for assessment are seen in the adolescent's pattern of conduct. Rather than classification of the disorder according to the underlying conflict, the diagnoses are based on the manifest symptom, that of violating societal and age-appropriate norms. The three different subheadings in this category are arranged according to whether or not the pattern of conduct has occurred as a group activity.

The *DSM-III-R* describes clear behavioral criteria for this diagnosis. It explains that to be diagnosed in this category, the adolescent must exhibit a repetitive pattern of behavior which violates the rights of others and major age-appropriate societal norms. Examples given include physical violence or theft that involves confrontation of the victim. Within this diagnosis the *DSM-III-R* differentiates between adolescents who are socially isolated and adolescents who claim loyalty to members of their group.

In his discussion of antisocial behavior, Malmquist (1978) gives a clearer picture of the adolescent most likely to be placed in this diagnostic category. He describes the tension-discharge personality disorder in terms of the adolescent's difficulties with impulse control, his/her shallow relationships with others and a low frustration tolerance. He relates this disorder to his discussion of the adolescent's defensive structure by pointing out how this kind of disorder is psychodynamically related to the adolescent's defective ego's attempt to cope with age-related tasks:

> Denial of dependency needs, strong reaction formations against these needs by exaggerated independence, projection of hostility onto others, and rationalizations for their behavior are rampant. (p. 630)

Figure 9, a fourteen-year-old girl's collage, clearly depicts the kind of disorder just described. The collage was created early in art psychotherapy treatment when the therapist requested that the adolescent select two pictures, one that represented herself as others saw her and one that represented herself as she felt inside. The lack of insight which is characteristic of adolescents diagnosed with undersocialized aggressive conduct disorder was in evidence with this girl, who declined to discuss her collage, simply stating that she "liked the pictures." Despite the girl's denial, the artwork speaks clearly about the intrapsychic conflicts behind the symptomatic behavior that led to her diagnosis. The cornered tiger on the left side of the page is a poignant portrayal of her aggressive reactions to the powerless feelings created by her difficulties with early object relations. In this case, the girl appeared to be involved in delinquent activity (theft and vandalism) as a way of discharging the psychodynamic tensions centered around an ambivalent connection with her mother. On the right side of the page, she unguardedly expressed her feelings of alienation, isolation and vulnerability. In this section of the art piece it is easy to see how the art therapy modality can simultaneously allow expressive and defensive outlets.

Although the adolescent's collage picture selection suggests a willingness to explore her feelings, she immediately picked up the markers and compulsively detailed a large border around the magazine picture as a way of defending against this potential self-disclosure. In this one art production, it is possible for the art therapist (and of course for the patient) to witness the integration of the behavioral and the psychody-

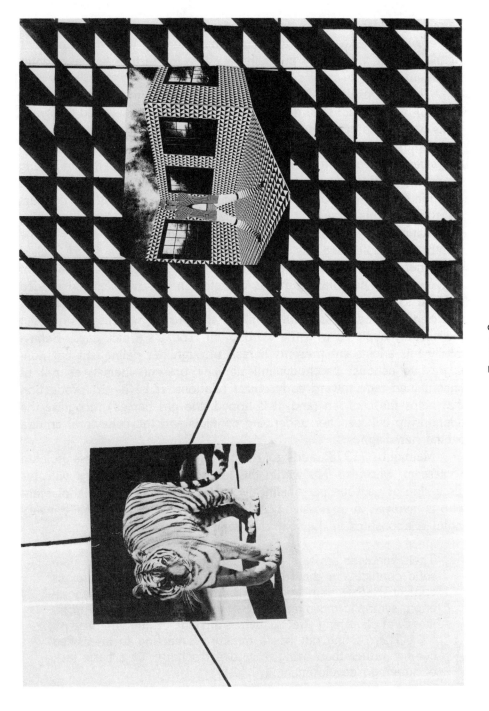

Figure 9

namic aspects of this conduct disorder. The art modality allows the expression of the symptom to occur simultaneously with the expression of the conflict, potentially providing a guide for further insight-oriented treatment.

The next example discusses a less aggressive manifestation of the *DSM-III-R*'s Conduct Disorder diagnosis, illustrating how varied the symptoms within this category can be.

Figure 10 is a drawing created by a fifteen-year-old girl placed in a residential treatment center after several years of peripheral gang involvement. Her chronic truancy, her disregard for authority and her isolation from peers contributed to her descriptive diagnosis as conduct disorder. In this drawing, a great deal of the intrapsychic material underlying her symptomatic expression is obvious. At the center of the picture the adolescent has drawn the self-representative figure locked out of her windowless and apparently inaccessible house. Her ambivalent relationship to parental figures is depicted in the perplexingly shaded sun and simultaneously weeping cloud. The figure itself stands defiantly, fists clenched and dressed boldly in red and purple, nonetheless denying the hostility depicted with the words, "Hi. Today's a nice day." Behaviorally this adolescent presents herself through her delinquent but non-aggressive actions; psychodynamically she presents herself as full of uncontained rage toward early object relations. It is the art production that helps the clinician (and, it is hoped, the girl herself) recognize the relationship between her underlying conflicts and the behavioral criteria behind her diagnosis.

Malmquist (1978) adds to the understanding of the less isolated adolescent, who also falls within this large diagnostic category, with his discussion of neurotic personality disorders. He describes the adolescent who is involved in aggressive conduct but capable of emotionally meaningful relationships in the following manner:

> Their behavior appears more characteristic of repressed neurotic conflicts, in that they repeat a pattern of unconscious conflict. Rather than tending toward pure discharge phenomenon, symbolic meaning may be in evidence. A greater prominence of disturbing affects, such as anxiety, or guilt are present. . . . Their acting out has a quality of reacting to intensified conflict rather than being a sudden discharge or a basic lack of superego development. (p. 631)

Figure 10

Figure 11, a drawing created by a seventeen-year-old girl, is an excellent pictorial representation of the dynamics that are often at the root of the diagnosis of conduct disorder. Although this drawing was produced well after a strong therapeutic alliance had been established, it provides an example of how the art therapy modality can help a troubled adolescent crystallize the expression of his/her conflicts. The drawing was originally produced without the titles at the top of the page. It was created as a response to the therapist's request that the girl illustrate herself both "in and out of trouble." The drawings, an ignited time bomb on the left side ("out of trouble") and an angry explosion on the right side ("in trouble"), speak clearly about this adolescent's conflicts with control. In an attempt to harness the adolescent's capacity for insight, limited but greater than that of the adolescents already discussed in this chapter, the therapist asked her to title each side of the page, including the word "feelings" in both titles. The words were intended to provide a bridge between the pictorial (primary process) expression of conflict and its cognitive (secondary process) acknowledgment.

The self-portrait in Figure 12 was created by a fourteen-year-old boy diagnosed within the category of conduct disorder. The drawing provides many clues into the intrapsychic origins of the behaviors which contributed to this diagnosis. In an obvious manner, the self-representative figure embodies the repressed conflicts manifested in the artist's lying and truant behavior, which he exhibited despite continued attachment to parental figures. The boy depicted himself wearing a traditional shirt (typically worn by his father) even accentuating the emblem (a quality clothing logo), but he retained a hair and beard style detested by his family. His sense of isolation from the family, a defensive retreat from the distressing ambivalence, is symbolized in the drawing by the impossibility for eye contact through the sunglasses. In addition, the boy holds a can of beer in the drawing, a symbol of the manner in which he particularly provokes his parents' reactions. A drawing that contains this kind of intrapsychic clarification and so clearly represents the defensive maneuvers behind the boy's symptoms is a valuable tool in ongoing treatment.

Oppositional Defiant Disorder

This disorder is defined in the *DSM-III-R* as characterized by disobedient, negativistic and provocative opposition to authority figures

Figure 11

(parents and teachers). It includes a continually confrontive quality but is differentiated from the Conduct Disorders by not involving patterns of behavior which violate the rights of others. Malmquist (1978) illustrates the defensive nature of this disorder in his comparison of the oppositional personality to the compulsive personality. He suggests their dynamic similarities by pointing out their manifest differences:

> The main difference is the more open expression of hostility in the form of negativism, in contrast to the blunting seen in compulsive defenses. . . . Under a guise of conformity, these youths subtly provoke conflicts. (p. 625)

Figure 13 was created by a fifteen-year-old girl whose minor drug and alcohol abuse appeared to be a behavioral manifestation of oppo-

31

Figure 12

Figure 13

sitional defiant disorder. Drugs and alcohol were not used by this adolescent primarily as escape mechanisms but rather as attention-seeking provocative behavior intended to provide a release for her internal conflicts. The fact that drugs played a symptomatic role here is an important point: adolescent drug and alcohol abuse often can be understood as behavior that is part of a larger diagnostic syndrome. In this case, the young girl toyed with the abusive substances as a well-chosen method of provoking her parents.

ANXIETY DISORDERS OF ADOLESCENCE

Separation Anxiety Disorder

The *DSM-III-R* describes this disorder in terms of the behavioral manifestation of excessive anxiety around separation from major attachment figures. The *Manual* explains that despite the adolescent's possible denial of overconcern in this area, his/her uncomfortable behavior usually reflects the anxiety. Malmquist (1978) further elucidates the psychodynamics behind this disorder in his discussion of the passive dependent personality. He describes the type of adolescent who has had difficulty achieving independence and asserting initiative. He goes on to explain this developmental conflict in terms of an adaptive compromise between conflicting needs. It is helpful to understand how the adolescent diagnosed with separation anxiety disorder holds on to old behaviors that have in the past secured rewards as a way of maintaining control. Malmquist (1978) explains:

> Their inhibitions appear related to difficulties in maintaining control, or at least a fear of losing control should they not retain their passivity or gross inhibitions. (p. 624)

Figure 14 is a collage created by a seventeen-year-old girl diagnosed with separation anxiety disorder. The collage was produced in response to the therapist's suggestion that the adolescent select a picture to focus her confused verbal expression. She had begun the session distraught over an argument she had had with her mother and was unable to discuss her feelings. The process of selecting the collage picture helped her regain control and provided both the adolescent and the therapist with valuable clues into the dynamics behind her distress. The collage

34

Figure 14

reflects this girl's defensive regression to a preadolescent stage. The captions which she included in the collage suggest her conflicts with feelings of guilt. The picture provides graphic representation of her valiant struggles to defend against attachments to early object relations despite her maladaptive regressive solutions.

Avoidant Disorder of Adolescence

This disorder, as described in the *DSM-III-R,* is characterized by persistent and excessive shrinking from contact with strangers while simultaneously desiring continued intense inclusion within the family. This disorder usually involves behavior that severely interferes with social functioning and impedes the progress of developmentally important tasks. Psychodynamically this disorder is not unlike separation anxiety disorder in terms of the exaggeration of the regressive defensive maneuver.

Figures 15 and 16 are collages produced by a fifteen-year-old girl experiencing tremendous difficulties forming peer relationships and establishing age-appropriate functioning. Examined together, these two art productions depict the internal struggles this adolescent was experiencing as she defended against her anxiety with regressive attempts to avoid extrafamilial involvement. Both the collages were created during the same session as free-choice art projects. It is important to point out how this girl enjoyed and repeatedly used a particular process in art psychotherapy: beginning a picture with selected magazine pictures she would embellish the collage to complete the production. Figure 15 suggests the girl's wish to return to a nurtured infancy. She described the baby as "well cared for by expert gardeners." Figure 16 depicts the other side of this adolescent's regressive wishes, that is, her anxiety over the development of age-appropriate autonomy. In this production she pictures a teenage girl water-skiing, pulled through very turbulent water by two peers who are not adequately attentive to her difficulties. The anxiety in this picture, powerfully displayed in the line quality with which she drew the water, is a strong testament to the psychic reasons for the regressive yearnings of the earlier collage. When asked to examine the two pictures side by side at the end of the session in which they were created, the young artist remarked, "I guess they're both kind of me, huh?" The two productions were a valuable aid in helping this girl understand the reasons for her social difficulties.

Figure 15

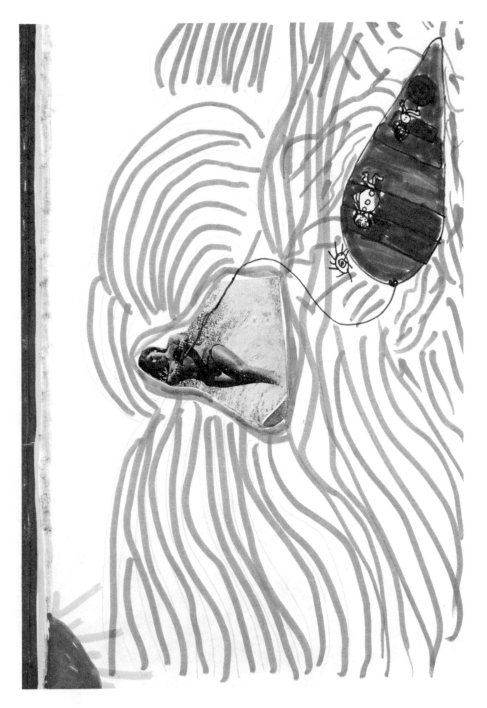

Figure 16

Overanxious Disorder

In this final disorder to be discussed in this category, the *DSM-III-R* continues its behavioral orientation. The *Manual* describes the adolescent diagnosed with this disorder as one who worries excessively and demonstrates fearful behavior. Typically the youngster is riddled with insecurities around his/her competence and often displays perfectionistic tendencies, obsessional self-doubt and nervous habits. Malmquist (1978) enriches the clinical understanding of this disorder in his discussion of the compulsive personality. He explains the behavioral manifestation in terms of the underlying defensive reactions to the anxiety so easily out of control in this developmental stage:

> Anxiety is experienced when the overcontrolled system fails and they cannot carry out their customary orderly behaviors. When that occurs, others in the environment may be perceived as responsible for their distress. . . . Contrary to a frequent picture of the compulsive personality as a rigid conformist, periodically releases occur by acting out. (p. 621)

Figure 17, a free-choice marker drawing created by a fifteen-year-old girl, clearly illustrates the symptomatic manifestations of this disorder. The adolescent spent the entire session compulsively detailing the explosions in this drawing. It appeared that she was attempting, on an unconscious level, to express, contain and organize her internal impulses. When the therapist reflected on this apparent dynamic, questioning the girl about the energy required to control the "outbursts" on the paper, the girl's defenses failed. The very subtle interpretation counteracted the compulsive efforts to contain the impulses and the girl bolted from the session before completing the picture.

OTHER DISORDERS OF ADOLESCENCE

Identity Disorder

Although by definition the developmental stage of adolescence is composed of identity struggles and confusion, with certain adolescents the internal reorganization that must be accomplished is severely stressful. The *DSM-III-R* describes this disorder as an extreme reaction to the tasks

Figure 17

of adolescence. The *Manual* defines identity disorder as the manifestations of severe subjective distress regarding an inability to reconcile aspects of the self into a relatively coherent and acceptable sense of self. This distress may involve decisions around careers, goals, sexual orientation, religion, moral values or group loyalties. Malmquist (1978) adds to the definition of this disorder as a particular crisis of adolescence. He discusses identity confusion as a constant for all youngsters but potentially a cause of maladaptive functioning for some. He points out the hazards along the way for adolescents attempting to come to terms with their own identity:

> There are then tendencies to diffusion, in time, appearance, action, personal inhibition, a searching for leaders who can resolve ambivalence by authoritarian solutions, a constant struggle against the world of technology and competition, and a discrepancy between what is viewed as dangerous in one's internal world and the actual dangers of the world. (Malmquist, 1978, p. 390)

Figure 18 is a collage created by a sixteen-year-old girl diagnosed with identity disorder. This adolescent appeared to be caught between conflicting wishes: a yearning to remain innocently childlike and a desire to become an impulsive and sexual adolescent whose impulses were both attractive and terrifying. Although her behavior was not troublesome, her intense confusion about dress, makeup, friends and social activities prohibited age-appropriate functioning. It appears that this girl's confusion was a defensive maneuver unconsciously designed to avoid the anxiety that autonomous functioning would cause. This collage powerfully displays the split this adolescent was experiencing, caught between the little girl she was and the woman she had yet to become. Art productions such as these can be used successfully to help the artist understand the core of his/her conflicts.

EATING DISORDERS

Eating disorders have become tragically common among adolescents. Although the psychodynamic orientation of this volume maintains that the eating disorder is most likely a symptom of a larger underlying dysfunction, these disorders are worthy of specific mention. Art therapy is being used successfully with adolescent anorectics/bulimics and the

Figure 18

Figure 19

reader is referred to the list of references provided by Wolf et al. (1985) for further study.

Anorexia Nervosa

The *DSM-III-R* lists an intense fear of becoming obese and a disturbance of body image as the most significant characteristics of this disorder. The current theoretical perspective on anorexia nervosa suggests that this disorder represents an attempt to solve a psychological conflict with a physical resolution: the concrete manipulation of intake and body shape. Wolf, Willmuth, Gazda and Watkins (1985) point out the relationship between the concrete solutions and the central issue of the anorectic as an early (preverbal) conflict over separation/individuation:

> If one conceptualizes the anorectic as operating partially on this level (nonverbal, kinesthetic/somatic and spatial), her attempts to solve abstract issues concretely, in a desperate attempt at mastery and the avoidance of shame, makes intrinsic sense. (p. 198)

Figure 19 is a collage/drawing created by a fourteen-year-old anorectic patient. In her own words, it represents her attempts to "get out from my depression." Significantly the girl selected a picture of a latency-age child eating eagerly as a self-representation. She embellished the picture with a containing eyeball surrounded by anxious markings and lightning bolts. This image suggests the relationship between the intrapsychic dynamics and the physical solution (defense against anxiety). Eating has apparently become a behavior that prevents acknowledgment of an internal process that probably is too threatening to be exposed. An art production as powerful as this one can be a tremendous aid in helping the adolescent begin to understand the dynamic nature of her symptoms.

The artwork in this chapter illustrates how the creative expression of the adolescent can provide access to the dynamics that underlie symptomatic behaviors. In this way the chapter introduces the manner in which adolescent artwork is interrelated with psychological disorders. The next section presents techniques and approaches that illustrate how treatment can proceed once the artwork is understood as primary communication.

3

Art Therapy Approaches with Adolescents

The focus in this chapter is on specific treatment guidelines that are sensitive to the unique ways that adolescents can make therapeutic use of the art experience. The establishment of the art thera-pist–adolescent client relationship is examined with a particular focus on transference issues, then the adolescent's expression is emphasized with a detailed analysis of art therapy directives and media as tools to help augment self-expressive attempts. Approaches that are responsive to the adolescent style and can be adapted for specific clinical use are suggested.

GENERAL ART THERAPY APPROACHES

Establishing the Relationship

It is important to understand the concept of transference as it is uniquely manifested by the adolescent patient. Since psychoanalytically oriented therapy depends on the development of a transferential relationship, it is worthwhile to examine the literature on this point. Contemporary clinicians concur that the transference response of the adolescent differs from the original understanding of this unique reexperiencing of early relationships within the therapeutic intimacy. Since the struggles of the adolescent involve separation from the early object relations, fully developed transference reactions that recreate the earlier relationships are both defended against (by the adolescent) and counterindicated (by the clinician). However, it is important for treatment that the therapeutic relationship be allowed to take on the distortions present in the adolescent's interactions with his/her parents. Consequently, a fine balance must be struck in the therapist's efforts to simultaneously limit and encourage transferential distortions. August Aichorn (1935, in Esman, 1983) suggests the appropriate approach in his discussion of social work with the dissocial adolescent:

> The worker becomes the father or the mother but still not wholly so; he represents their claims, but in the right moment he must let the dissocial child know that he has insight into his difficulties and that he will not interpret the behavior in the same way as the parents. (p. 9)

Creation of a productive and developmentally responsive therapeutic alliance, crucial in treatment with all populations, is particularly difficult with the adolescent patient. The adolescent's vague and anxious sense of self undercuts his/her desperate need for human identification patterns to restore a sense of direction. Consequently, the relationships in which he/she becomes involved are utilized primarily to restore psychic deficiencies. Esman (1983) explains the need for special techniques in the beginning stages of treatment with the emotionally disturbed adolescent:

> Perhaps the most taxing problem in the treatment of the severely disturbed adolescent is that of finding a channel for the establishment of a therapeutic relationship. Too old for the play techniques of early childhood, the adolescent has not yet evolved the cognitive and self-observing capacities that will permit him to use the free association approach of adult analytic therapy, and is, in any case, a frequently unwilling patient, oriented more to action than to reflection as a means of reducing tension and warding off anxiety. (p. 141)

Because of the power of art expression at this stage of development, as described in the previous two chapters, the adolescent's creative activity can be utilized to help the therapist with the initial establishment of a relationship. Art expression provides an excellent opportunity for the therapist to avoid typical early obstacles in the treatment of adolescents. It channels the adolescent's natural propensities and provides a vehicle for the therapist to acquaint the adolescent with the therapeutic situation. Although recurrent waves of frustration will continue to threaten the therapeutic alliance all through treatment with adolescents, the disruptions can be mediated when the therapist's technique demonstrates sensitivity to the client's progressive development. Open-ended art directives, intended to encourage the youngster to introduce himself/herself to the therapist in ego-syntonic ways, are the most effective tools in the early stages of art therapy treatment.

Figure 1 presents a collage created by a seventeen-year-old girl in her first art therapy session. The piece was produced after the therapist introduced the girl to the art materials and encouraged her to select a medium to explain something about who she was. Like many adolescents, she chose collage, a nonthreatening medium that provides a safe and structured resource in the difficult self-expressive process. The actual activity of sorting through the available pictures, gluing them on the paper and writing captions can help the youngster bind the anxiety created by the potential for self-disclosure. At the same time, the process introduces the adolescent to the idea that his/her art productions will become a vehicle for shared communication. The kind of initial experience evidenced in this collage can itself become valuable therapeutic material, but it is more important in helping the adolescent over the initial anxiety and consequent resistances to the therapeutic relationship.

In Figure 1, the collage process offered the artist a vehicle for a powerful message about her ambivalence; her poignant expression of pain ("Sometimes I feel I am being crushed by hurt") and her simultaneous warnings that these feelings are not immediately available for examination ("My feelings are sometimes like a streetlight"). The art modality was a productive way for this girl to approach treatment, giving her access to self-expression, allowing her to remain in control and providing her with a glimpse of her own potential for self-disclosure.

When the art productions are used to facilitate the treatment alliance, there is an impact on the type of transference distortions that result. In

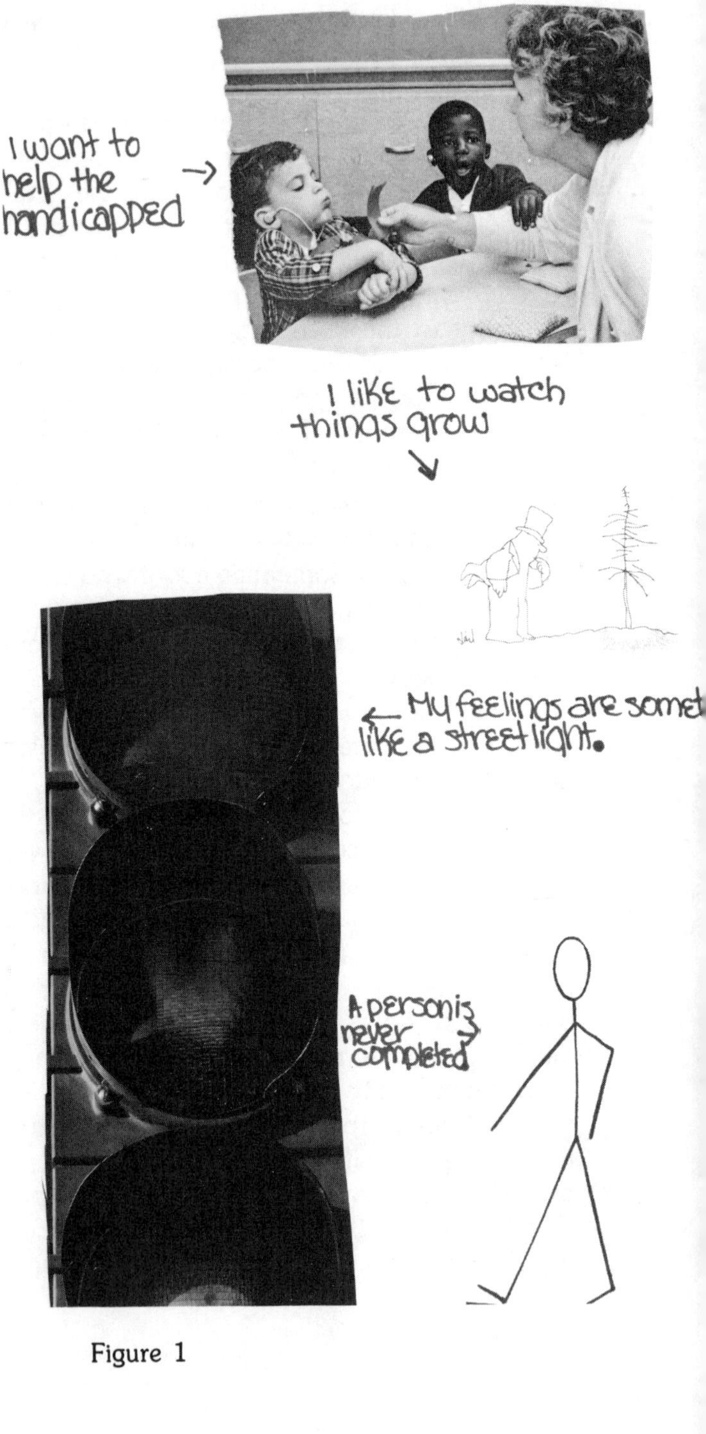

I want to
help the
handicapped →

I like to watch
things grow
↓

← My feelings are somet[...]
like a street light.

A person is
never
completed →

Figure 1

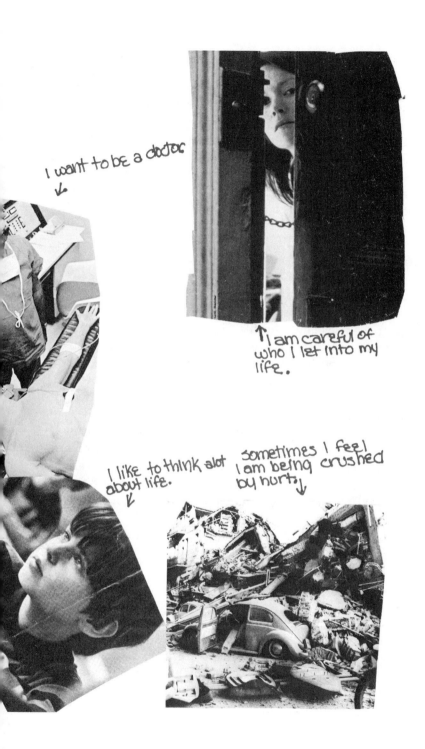

I want to be a doctor

I am careful of who I let into my life.

I like to think alot about life.

Sometimes I feel I am being crushed by hurt.

the art therapy relationships lies the inherently nurturing interaction of providing art supplies. For an adolescent whose childhood was complicated with difficulties around nurturance, this unlimited availability of materials biases the establishment of a therapeutic relationship. In some ways the bias is helpful to treatment, allowing the adolescent to feel replenished and possibly more amenable to therapeutic involvement. In other ways the bias is troublesome, creating an immediate transference distortion and possibly flooding the youngster with overstimulation. Consequently, the art modality must be understood as a powerful tool in the early stages of treatment and not underestimated as a simple method of eliciting information.

Accepting Expression

It is imperative that the art therapist accept all early attempts at self-expression. Frequently the adolescent's fears and anxieties will cause initial efforts to appear defensive, even hostile. These types of productions, exemplified by Figure 2, are important expressions and valuable communications at this early stage in treatment.

Figure 2, a pastel drawing created by a fourteen-year-old girl, appears to be a simple cataloguing of favorite rock groups and stars. Understood, however, as a defensive maneuver against the encouragement for self-disclosure inherent in the art therapy modality, it is an important expression. The drawing, somewhat manic in color and style, clearly portrays the artist's anxiety and fragility. Not ready yet to take risks with self-expression, this adolescent utilized the art supplies in a defensive manner. Unconditionally accepted and saved in a drawing folder for future reference, this art production recorded the adolescent's early resistances, simultaneously allowing her to enter into an alliance with the therapist who provided the experience.

Facilitating the Expansion of Self-Expression

When the art modality is effectively used to help establish the treatment alliance, many of the initial difficulties inherent in therapy with adolescents are minimized. As therapy proceeds, the art productions can continue to be used as aids in the obstacle-ridden process. The most significant function of the creative process, once the therapeutic relationship has been developed, is in augmenting tentative attempts at self-

50

Figure 2

expression. Figure 3 is an example of how the art process can respond to spontaneously executed but limited expression, encouraging its development into fuller, therapeutically meaningful material.

Figure 3 began as a marker drawing of an eye, flooding over with tears and heavily embellished with eye makeup. The artist, a fifteen-year-old girl, had been in art therapy for several weeks, but up to this time had created only stereotypic posters of favorite rock groups, not unlike the drawing in Figure 2. With the spontaneous switch to the more self-expressive symbol seen in the upper right portion of Figure 3, the girl indicated her willingness to progress, however cautiously, in the direction that the art materials (and the accepting art therapy relationship) were encouraging. What was required was a structuring directive that could focus and augment the material suggested in the tearful eye. The technique of the art therapist at this point is crucial; he/she must assess the defensive style of the adolescent, analyze the adolescent's preparation for expanding self-expression, and be prepared for the adolescent's regressive retreat. With all these factors in mind, the art therapist can offer an art directive that will utilize the tentative expression to elicit the repressed material that has come to be evident under the surface of previous art productions.

In this example, the art therapist suggested that the girl illustrate "a drop from the tearful eye." Responding to this challenge to augment her symbol, the artist drew the circle under the eye, then added and crossed out the word "HATE." She explained that her hateful feelings "make me sad" and proceeded to label the victims of her negative feelings around the page: "mom," "stepbrother," "dad," "stepdad" and "brother." Apparently agitated by the angry outburst, she quickly added that she also felt a "lot of love," drew the word "LOVE" to the left of the eye, and added family members "sister" and "aunt" to the constellation. In essence, the drawing represents the tremendous ambivalence this youngster feels toward her family and the series of abandonments which she had experienced as a member of this dysfunctional unit. It illustrates how a directed art experience can facilitate the expansion of self-expressive attempts when the art modality has already established a treatment alliance.

It is significant that the drawing in Figure 3 resembles all the artwork this girl had done previously—all in red, all incorporating block letter words scattered over the page. This resemblance hints at the slow pace of therapeutic progress. Although the artist is suggesting her capacity

Figure 3

to utilize the art modality for direct self-expression, she remains poised to retreat back the short distance to the rock posters. It is up to the art therapist to sensitively sustain the augmentation without catalyzing a regressive retreat. Throughout this difficult process, the artwork itself supplies a clear indication of the adolescent's response to the therapist's techniques.

Responding to Underlying Meanings

The role of interpretation in art therapy is a complicated one and varies from one practitioner to another. With an adolescent population, the value of an interpretive art therapy approach is particularly controversial. It is the intent of this section to demonstrate art therapy techniques that avoid the problems with interpretation but accomplish similar results. It is important to understand the art therapy efforts in the context of "working through therapies." Malmquist (1978) provides an excellent explanation of insight-oriented work with adolescents:

> Working through therapies seek to go beyond efforts at symptom removal or environmental clarification. They seek clarification of conscious conflicts and resolution of unconscious processes which have been operating antithetically to development. Merely pointing these out to an adolescent . . . has little effect . . . the goal is to achieve structural change so that different adaptive techniques can be used in interaction with the environment. For the adolescent, in particular, this reorganization seeks to alter developmental distortions and arrests so that ego and superego development may progress. (p. 865)

Typically such an approach relies on interpretation as an important technique in fulfilling its goals. For example, as the adolescent expression emerges, in behavior, in words or in fantasies, the psychodynamically oriented therapist attempts to guide the adolescent toward an understanding of the repressed component of his/her experience. Because of the adolescent's yet undeveloped ego and weak superego these interpretive efforts can be destructive to the youngster's fragile psychic structure. Alternative approaches to the identical goal of "making the unconscious, conscious" are available within the art therapy modality. Figure 4 (discussed previously as Figure 8 in Chapter 2) and Figure 5 illustrate how an art directive can function in place of an interpretation to help the client explore latent material.

Figure 4 is a marker drawing created by a fifteen-year-old boy whose father had recently died of cancer. The drawing was produced spontaneously, compulsively executed with a ruler and pencil and then colored with markers. The drawing itself suggests the boy's isolation and the defenses he employs in response to his recent suffering. (See the discussion in Chapter 2 for an analysis of the defensive style evident in this drawing.) It is the boy's verbal description of the picture that most poignantly suggests its intrapsychic significance. He explained that "the mailman would not find the letter in the mailbox because of the high fence." It was clear from the metaphor developed in this drawing that the artist was harboring an important message, portrayed symbolically as a piece of mail. The boy's ambivalence about making his message available to others was also clear, suggested by his decision to fence in the mailbox. Apparently, the youngster's isolation and exacerbated defenses inhibited his ability to express and deal with his pain. It would have been premature to interpret the obvious but latent material in this powerful drawing. An interpretation which suggested the defensive maneuver so clearly depicted would have caused the boy to retreat even further from the tentative expression in this production. Instead an art directive was conceived to focus the boy's expressive efforts and encourage him to take a step toward fuller self-expression.

Remaining within the metaphor but seizing the symbol that appeared to be the boy's pivotal experience, the art therapist suggested he draw a representation of the content of the letter in the mailbox. Sensitive to the boy's agitation in response to this directive, the therapist provided structure for the task by offering the collage pictures as an alternative medium. Figure 5 is the boy's response to the directive and the encouraged switch of medium. The finished product suggests the youngster's conflicts over the recent death of his father. The collage is a powerful one, channeling the creative energy of a grieving adolescent into an expressive outlet. The process, without further discussion, was clearly therapeutic and the session was ended without further artwork. In response to both productions, alternatives to interpretation were selected as therapeutic interventions. After the first production (Figure 4) the art therapist chose to use an art directive to facilitate augmented self-expression, thereby harnessing the therapeutic power of the art process

55

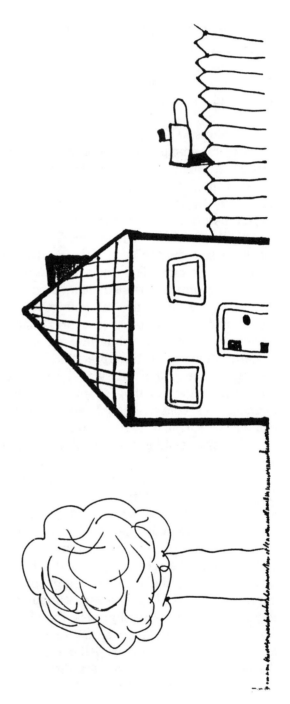

Figure 4

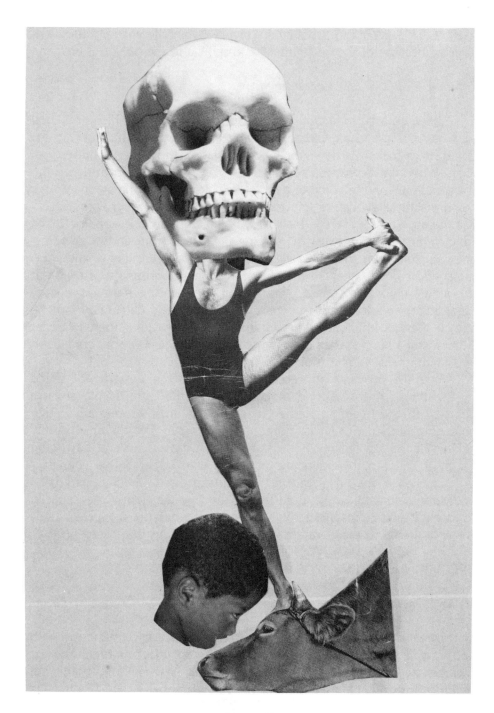

Figure 5

itself. After the second production (Figure 5) a different approach was selected because of the boy's affective response to the powerful imagery.

Offering Empathy and Encouragement

When an art production depicts, for the first time, difficult material that has not yet been verbalized, it is countertherapeutic for the art therapist to focus his/her efforts on translating the material into verbal form. When the expression retains a defensive quality, appearing incomplete and only on the verge of genuine self-exploration, the art therapist's responsibilities involve structuring art tasks to catalyze growth in self-expression (see Figure 4). However, when the artwork appears to be truly original for the artist, a genuine departure from earlier defenses, encouragement for further creative endeavors is insensitive to the enormous efforts just witnessed (see Figure 5). The appropriate response at this time is empathy. The art therapist must respect the enormous energy required for an adolescent to depart from rigidly held defenses. Empathy can be offered within and without the metaphor, providing the adolescent with an empathic response both to the latent feelings in the art production and to the risks he/she took in its execution.

Figure 5 provides an excellent example of an opportunity seized by the therapist to respond empathically to the intrapsychic stresses depicted in the imagery. Rather than making an interpretation or encouraging further creative exploration of the issue, the therapist simply acknowledged the feelings. The statement "Death is a very hard thing for most children to understand and deal with" offered this youngster the knowledge that his feelings, still unexpressed directly, had been understood. It would take time before the boy developed the capacity to openly discuss his grief, but it was clear that his art productions (Figures 4 and 5) were important steppingstones in that direction.

SPECIFIC ART THERAPY TECHNIQUES

Using Directives

Directives play a very important role in art psychotherapy with adolescents, functioning as catalysts for therapeutic progress. The art therapist who understands their full potential can skillfully guide the treatment process. Figure 6 demonstrates how an open-ended art directive

58

can facilitate the type of spontaneous self-expression that is most helpful in the early stages of treatment with adolescents. Figure 7 demonstrates how a very specific art directive that arises out of previous art productions can focus an adolescent's self-expression. Figure 8 demonstrates how directives can be conceived to aid the adolescent's acceptance of re-sponsibility for therapeutic progress. The three examples included in this section are certainly not exhaustive; rather, they were chosen to illustrate how specific treatment goals can be translated into art tasks. This concept is at the core of the art therapy modality. With a thorough understanding of the adolescent stage of development, an accurate analysis of the defensive style and psychopathology of the particular client and an experienced appreciation of the art process, the art therapist can direct the adolescent's progress toward improved intrapsychic functioning. The following examples illustrate the role that art directives play in this process.

Figure 6 is a collage and marker drawing created by a fifteen-year-old girl who was very resistant to participation in the art therapy modality. Claiming that art tasks were "babyish" and "a waste of time," she habitually avoided eye contact with the art therapist and drummed her fingers anxiously on the table. It was obvious that this youngster was terrified of the potential for self-disclosure and intimacy evident in the therapy sessions. Although she had been told that the art materials were available for use in whatever way she chose, she had so far resisted engaging in both the treatment relationship and the art process. The art therapist elected to utilize an open-ended directive to help the girl become involved in a creative endeavor. Since undirected spontaneous partici-pation appeared to be too threatening to this adolescent, structure and limits were built into the task. When the girl was asked to simply choose a magazine picture that she liked and embellish it on the paper in any way she wanted, she was able for the first time to become involved in the session. Figure 6 depicts the finished product that arose out of the directive. In it the adolescent suggests her impoverished emotional ex-perience and low self-esteem. In the story she was encouraged to write on the side of the page, the adolescent gives clues to her affective life. Despite the fact that the girl denied her own sadness, in the metaphor created in this art production she was able to acknowledge the feelings behind her "boredom" in the persona of "Sandy." Because this drawing was created very early in treatment and because it was an important departure from her rigid defenses, the symbolism was not explored.

59

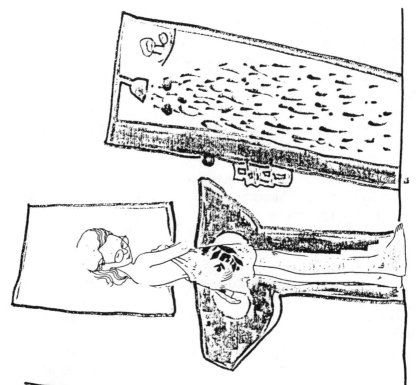

one morning sandy
got up. she felt very
sad, she went in the
bathroom to take a
shower. But she
still felt sad.
she missed her
parents and she
knew that even
if her boyfriend
came she would
still miss her
parents. she
wished she
had somebody
to talk to.
But she knew
she would
just go to school
and be bored

Figure 6

Instead, the effort to become involved with the art experience was reinforced. Augmentation and focusing of the self-expression would wait for a time later in treatment when more specific art directives could be utilized without causing the defensive retreat that would likely occur at this early stage.

Figure 7, a marker drawing created by a seventeen-year-old girl, illustrates a more complex use of the art therapy directive to focus self-exploration. Prior to the execution of this drawing, the adolescent had used her art therapy sessions only to create abstract drawings that represented her moods. As she developed her style of self-expression, a pattern developed in which she began her imagery with angular black lines but progressively obscured them with colorful scribbles. As this pattern became increasingly ritualized, it was apparent that the resulting imagery paralleled the defensive maneuvers in which she obscured her feelings of anger and depression with a well-developed denial system.

The art therapist encouraged her to explore the meaning of this pattern with a specific art directive. Suggesting that she divide a page into halves, the art therapist provided an opportunity for the adolescent to separate the expressive from the defensive material that had habitually appeared in her previous drawings. To continue the theme of separating the affect from the defense, the girl was directed to unravel the black portions of her typical imagery from the pastel portions. The resulting drawing, this adolescent's first attempt at representation in art therapy, is very revealing. The tightly sealed jar, drawn in black, on the left side of the page contains expressions of anger that the youngster claimed were directed at "no one in particular." The brightly colored flowers on the right side of the page are surrounded by anxious-looking scribbles that appear to confine the three blossoms. The artist described this section of the drawing as "pretty, not depressing like the other side."

The two-part drawing provides a clear depiction of the youngster's two-part internal process: on one side the anger and depression that exacerbate the separation conflicts of adolescence, and on the other side the defensive response to the consequent anxiety. Although this girl was not yet ready to explore the origins of her debilitating anger, this drawing demonstrated the therapeutic progress she had made. The well-timed and sympathetic directive had helped her isolate and begin to identify the feelings that had previously been inseparable from her denial system.

Figure 8 is a collage created by a fifteen-year-old girl who was seen only briefly in art therapy. Knowing that the adolescent's involvement

Figure 7

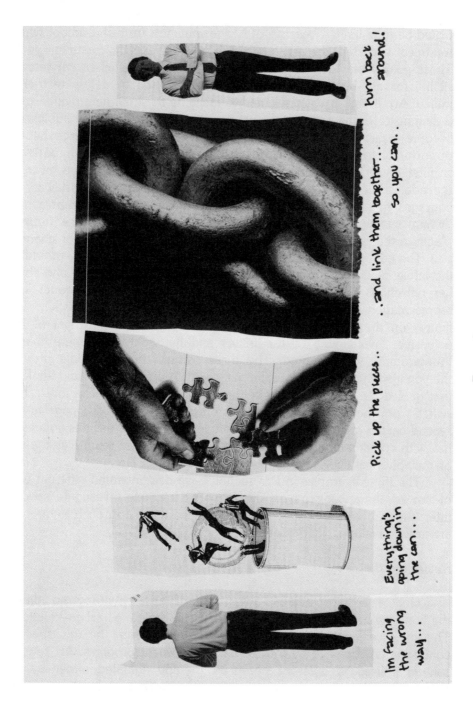

Figure 8

would be time limited because of her termination from the school where treatment occurred, the art therapist established specific treatment goals. These goals were focused around helping the youngster accept responsibility for her behavior as she made a transition to a less restrictive milieu. Art directives were selected to facilitate the treatment plan. Figure 8 demonstrates the power of an art directive to help a reticent adolescent become engaged in treatment issues. The art modality offered her an opportunity to participate in an age-appropriate activity with potential to filter issues out of unfocused verbal material. The directive given to the adolescent was simple but carefully thought out: the girl was encouraged to select and position on the page pictures that represented "where she was now" and "where she wanted to be in the future," placing other selections between them to show the process of change.

The collage in Figure 8 took the entire session to create, providing the adolescent with an excellent opportunity to reflect silently and share her reflections as she wished. She explained her finished product as a representation of her "need to work things out with my family." The figures on the far right and far left are an accurate portrayal of her defensive "avoidance" of the issues and her acknowledgment that a "turnaround" was required. The three pictures in the middle provide the youngster with an explorable metaphor ("puzzle pieces" and "links") that guided her understanding of the process of change. The interesting switch from the first person pronoun on the left side of the page to the second person pronoun on the right suggests the difficulties this youngster has with contemplating the future directly and further reinforces the use of metaphorical self-expression.

The three examples in this section have demonstrated different uses of the art therapy directive. The following sections investigate specific interventions that are consistent with the theoretical approach to directed art tasks developed in this chapter.

Reviewing the Art

One of the most obvious advantages of the art therapy modality is the concrete record of treatment available in the saved art productions. The adolescent patient, particularly, can benefit from the retrospective confrontation provided by the review of treatment progress. Art reviews can be utilized at different points in therapy, initiated either by the therapist or the client. Most typically they are a tool for termination, focusing on the resolution of treatment issues.

Figure 9 is a graph produced by a fourteen-year-old girl as she retrospectively explored her art productions of twenty-two months. The chart underlying this graph was introduced as a method of structuring the process of review for this adolescent whose art production had been so prolific that the sheer volume was overwhelming. This framework was selected to help minimize the anxiety around analyzing material that depicted difficult experiences and demonstrated earlier maladaptive problems. As the artwork was examined in the order it was produced, the adolescent was encouraged to use the chart to evaluate the functioning level portrayed in her art. As the months were reviewed, the chart began to depict the tremendous oscillations she had experienced early in treatment and the moderating effect continued therapy had provided. As the girl confronted old self-expressive efforts, her progress became clearer and clearer. Consequently, the art productions themselves became concrete evidence of improvement and provided an opportunity for the important therapeutic task of reinforcing change.

Encouraging Journals

A technique related to the art review, but utilized on an ongoing basis rather than periodically or only at termination, is the imagery journal. This art task involves the adolescent in a continuous self-expressive effort that serves many functions. Blos (1962) articulates the developmental value of this type of task in his discussion of diaries:

> The diary still serves the same psychological purpose which consists in filling the emotional void felt when the novel instinctual drives of puberty can no longer be articulated on old objects and cannot yet be articulated on new objects, so that fantasy life assumes a most important and essential function. (p. 95)

In addition to helping the adolescent through the separation process, the journal encourages reflection, role playing and experimentation, thereby helping prevent acting out. Even extremely resistant adolescents are able to utilize the structure and framework provided by the imagery journal to experiment with self-expression. In each session the adolescents can be encouraged to select collage pictures or create simple marker drawings to be placed in journal folders and kept in chronological order. Although the artwork itself frequently is limited, the creation of an

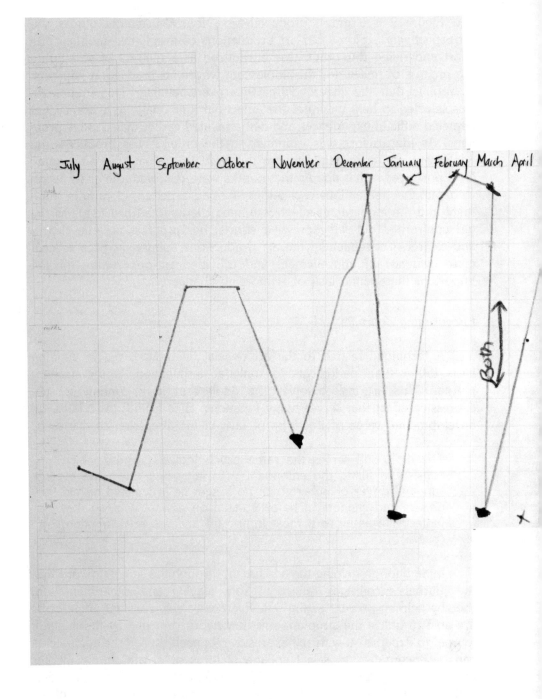

Figure 9

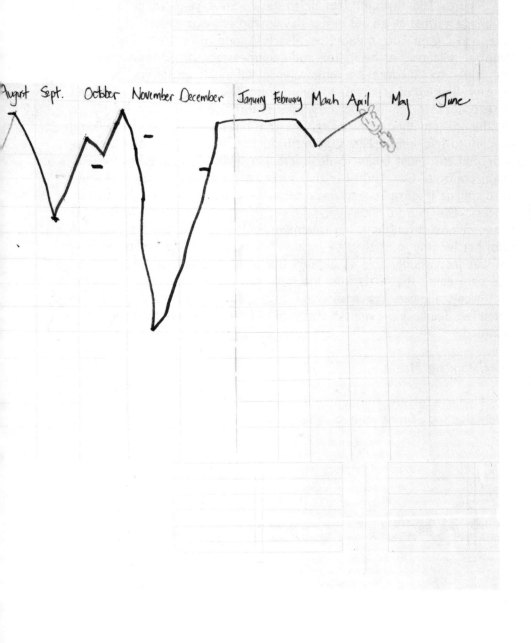
August Sept. October November December January February March April May June

ongoing cumulative expression becomes very powerful. In most cases, the adolescents grow attached to this project and are able to observe their own development in self-expression over time.

Figures 10*a* through 10*d* illustrate a sixteen-year-old girl's use of the image journal as an aid in her developing self-expression. The simple collage in Figure 10*a*, created on March 7 soon after the girl began art therapy, indicates her hesitation and eagerness about this new modality. She chose to illustrate her ambivalence with collage letters, retaining the most limiting of all media to help control the potential anxiety around self-exposure. In Figure 10*b*, created just three sessions later, on March 28, the girl remained with collage material but had progressed to adding imagery to her words. Her simple production suggests her own perceptions that she must begin to deal with her feelings despite her need to retain controls. On April 11, the adolescent reverted to an imageless word collage (Figure 10*c*) in response to her anxiety over the therapeutic process. The journal, however, allowed her to chart these feelings as they oscillated throughout her treatment. In Figure 10*d*, the last selection from her lengthy journal to be included here, the girl demonstrates how she was increasingly able to express her feelings in her simple collages. The very same materials and the very same structure provided week after week allowed the adolescent to produce a powerful journal in which her decreasing defenses and increasing self-expression were clearly recorded.

Understanding Media

Media selection frequently is neglected as a clinical issue in art psychotherapy. Since one of the important tasks of the clinical art

Opening new doors.

Figure 10*a*

Figure 10b

WHY AM I SO TIRED

Treat yourself

Charting the Changes

JOY...
GIVES
Spirit

The Reality Is Always Worse

Figure 10c

Figure 10d

therapist is guiding the client's participation in the art process, an understanding of the way particular materials can contribute to the process is essential. It is helpful to conceptualize the art materials in terms of a continuum from structured to nonstructured. Structured materials, such as collage material or pencils, limit clients in the way they can be used and offer little opportunity for regression or overstimulation. At the other end of the continuum are materials such as finger paints and wet clay, which provide the client with few inherent limits and offer an immediate opportunity to experience primary process. All of the materials can be understood to fit somewhere along this continuum, although their positions may differ for different kinds of populations. The art therapist needs to consider this continuum when selecting or encouraging materials for treatment. Obviously the medium should be chosen in response to the client's initial responses to the art experience and modified (or not modified) as his/her participation evolves. The following three examples illustrate the very important role that media selection plays in art psychotherapy, particularly with an adolescent population. Figure 11 demonstrates one of the reasons for the tremendous therapeutic value of collage material with this age group. Figures 12 and 13 portray the kinds of self-expressive experiences that can be provided for adolescents when alternative materials are considered.

Figure 11 is a collage produced by a fifteen-year-old girl who was very frightened by the potential for self-disclosure within the art modality. Unwilling to use the art materials for self-expression, she spent most of her sessions examining the pictures in the collage box, verbally sharing her projections about the imagery. This activity was channeled into a directive that was sensitive to her dependency on the already created imagery of the collage pictures. Encouragement of this particular adolescent to attempt her own personal expression independent of the magazine pictures would have been insensitive to her defensive style. However, the incorporation of her own medium selection into an intrapsychically challenging directive harnessed the potential of this somewhat limited material. The adolescent was encouraged to create several collages that depicted each of a list of "feelings" she developed with the therapist. Figure 11, the girl's portrayal of "depressed," demonstrates the power of the collage material to provide a structured opportunity for difficult material to be shared. In this collage, the girl expresses her shattered feelings regarding the recent institutionalization of her mother. Although this collage was ostensibly not created about her own feelings,

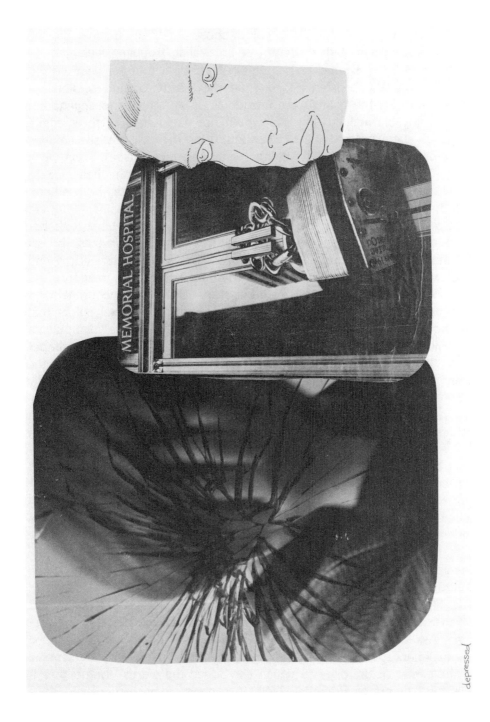

Figure 11

depressed

the distancing provided by the medium chosen and the directive allowed this adolescent a tentative attempt at unraveling troubling feelings.

Figure 12 is a tempera painting created by a fourteen-year-old girl who had initially resisted all the materials. After several sessions of noninvolvement the paints were introduced in an attempt to engage her in an enjoyable activity that she would not experience as threatening. Although she expressed skepticism about using the tempera, she enjoyed the process of setting up the paints, water can and brushes. Each week she set up the paints in a ritualistic manner, using the behavior to provide structure for her increasing experimentation with the medium Her first paintings were characterized by large amounts of paint splattered, dropped and blown. As she became increasingly comfortable with her involvement, the defensive brittleness with which she distanced the art therapist began to dissolve. Over time the girl was encouraged to find images in the shapes which appeared within the abstract imagery.

Figure 12 is a painting created in response to that encouragement. The project began as a swirling experiment with the pastel colors that the adolescent had spent half the session mixing. As she manipulated the thickly applied paint with her brush, she associated one of her shapes to a "teddy bear." When encouraged to include the teddy bear in the painting she quickly created the imagery seen in Figure 12 (originally without the heavily painted black lines that surround all the representations). She described the teddy bear's angry exclamation (upper right) as his response to finding the framed picture of his beloved pet cat (lower left) "cracked because of his father's carelessness."

With some direction the painting process had evolved from a loosening-up exercise to an opportunity for symbolic expression of repressed anger. With adolescents so terrified of self-exploration that their defensive rigidity prevents them from engaging in creative endeavors, unstructured art materials can be carefully introduced to offer a non-threatening entry into art expression. As Figure 12 illustrates, playful manipulation of a potentially expressive medium can facilitate its eventual utilization for genuine self-expression.

Figure 13 is the expression of a seventeen-year-old girl at the end of an art therapy session in which she had used wet clay for the first time. Asked to produce some kind of image on the paper to describe the experience, which she had enjoyed intensely, she created the scribble in the center of the page to which she added the words "Sometimes it was mud or art or Freudian. Now it is gone." The tactile experience

Figure 12

I PRAYED W/ CLAY TODAY.

SOMETIMES IT
WAS MUD OR

ART OR
FREUDIAN.
NOW IT IS GONE.

Figure 13

with the wet clay had been a powerful one for this adolescent, helping her find access to the kind of primary process usually denied her by her fortified defense system. In her play, she had spontaneously verbalized childlike fantasies of destruction and gleeful aggression. Although the intrapsychic material emerging from this regressive experience was not utilized directly, the process had provided the girl with nonretaliatory opportunity for expression. The adolescent responded to the encouragement for expression inherent in the medium and experienced the lowering of defense mechanisms required for effective psychotherapy. The art therapist insisted on a concrete product to record the experience (Figure 13) in order that this turning point in treatment remain available for retrospective review.

Three different materials have been included as examples in this discussion of the role of media in art psychotherapy with adolescents. They were selected as illustrations of three particular points along the structured–unstructured continuum. This continuum should be understood in terms of the ego functioning involved in the art processes stimulated by the material. At one end of the spectrum, collage was discussed as a particularly controlled and controllable medium, nonthreatening and responsive to the defensive needs of the adolescent. Paint and wet clay exemplified the other end of the spectrum, their regressive potential a powerful tool for the adolescent patient whose energies are directed at maintaining equilibrium. Although a wide variety of materials can and should be used in work with an adolescent population, it is helpful to understand their place in this continuum. With adolescents, encouragement and direction in media choice aids in the difficult task of remaining respectful toward necessary defenses while encouraging expressive growth. The art therapist's understanding of the significant impact made by the materials is a valuable treatment guide.

4

Two Case Examples

This chapter presents two case histories that demonstrate the treatment modality of art psychotherapy. The cases represent different points along the continuum of psychopathology and consequently illustrate different approaches to treatment. The two are contrasted and compared to convey the manner in which art expression can be harnessed to help adolescents master a variety of types of conflicts.

Material in this chapter is adapted from Greenspoon, D. Case Study: The Development of Self-Expression in a Severely Disturbed Adolescent. *American Journal of Art Therapy, 22*(1), 1982, by permission of Elinor Ulman and Vermont College of Norwich University; and Greenspoon, D. The Role of the Art Therapist as an Adjunctive Member of a Residential Treatment Team. *Residential Group Care and Treatment, 2*(3), 1984, by permission of Haworth Press.

CASE 1: CLIFF

Cliff was a fourteen-year-old Caucasian boy who was seen in individual art therapy for 30 months. His case stands as an excellent illustration of the effectiveness of this modality with adolescents capable of insight. A bright and artistically talented boy, Cliff made use of the art process as a tool to help him understand and compensate for early deficiencies in ego development.

Cliff's early development was dramatically affected by his father's departure when the boy was two years old. After this traumatic abandonment, Cliff grew increasingly close with his mother, becoming (in her words) "my only emotional outlet." When Cliff was seven years old and beginning what was to become a turbulent relationship with the public school system, his mother remarried. From the start Cliff experienced his stepfather as authoritarian, punitive and emotionally unavailable. After the marriage, Cliff's difficult adjustment to school worsened, his aggressive behavior problems exacerbated by the sudden "dethroning" as his mother's sole companion. The tenseness in the family constellation escalated over the next few years as two half-sisters were born. Acting-out behaviors increasingly became Cliff's defensive response to the intolerable impulses he was experiencing. The emotional abandonments he had suffered left him unprepared for a resurgence of separation issues and consequently his enraged outbursts increased at adolescence. The incident that finally precipitated police involvement and placement in the facility where art therapy treatment took place was Cliff's sexual molestation of his two half-sisters. This behavior, a desperate cry for help in mastering his impulses, initiated a series of psychotherapeutic interventions. It was art therapy, however, that provided Cliff with the opportunity for channeling his behavioral outbursts into symbolic expression in a way that he could understand and integrate.

Cliff's thirty-month participation in art therapy is condensed here. Although he produced a large number of artworks, only 12 have been included to illustrate his treatment. The 12 pieces were selected because they depict milestones or significant plateaus that Cliff reached as he struggled with self-expression. Each of the productions is analyzed as a reflection of his growing capacity to explore and understand his internal conflicts. In addition to the analysis of the artwork, the discussion outlines the approach and techniques used by the art therapist to facilitate Cliff's remarkable progress.

Cliff was excited about his referral to art therapy. He had been doing poorly in the traditional psychotherapy offered by the residential treatment center and his social worker believed that the art modality might help him past the obstacles they were both experiencing.

In his first art therapy session, Cliff responded eagerly to the variety of materials offered and immediately elected to use the Plasticine. He rapidly created a sculpture (not shown here) that he titled "Fast Food" in which a hamburger, a bag of French fries and a soda sit on a tray. This production not only indicated that Cliff experienced the art supplies as nurturance (not unusual with psychically wounded adolescents) but also suggested that a positive treatment alliance would not be difficult to create. Cliff spent the first several sessions experimenting with all the media available in the art therapy room, enthusiastically exhausting the supplies and then expressing anger toward the art therapist for not having "more." It was clear that the youngster's anger and ambivalence toward the providing adult related more to his early history than to the treatment relationship. Rather than attempt to analyze and explore this transference distortion (a tactic that would likely have caused a counterproductive reaction of anxiety and defenses), the art therapist continued to encourage spontaneous self-expression, confident that this important dynamic would surface in the art productions themselves.

Figure 1 is a pencil drawing that Cliff created in the second month of art therapy. It is a graphic representation of the boy's struggles with aggressive and dependent longings and a manifestation much more available for exploration than the behavior previously discussed. Cliff's struggles, which had originated in the problematic separation–individuation process with his mother, were behind both Cliff's distorted responses to the art therapist as the provider/withholder of materials and the content of this drawing. Cliff described the picture as "a turtle who is snapping at the hand that feeds it" and spent the remainder of the session discussing this creature. He seemed surprised when the turtle's quandary was compared with his own ambivalence in art therapy; did he want to make use of the art supplies more than he wanted to create reasons to become angry at the art therapist? After puzzling over this observation with Cliff, the art therapist continued to encourage communication primarily through the art process. Although some directed exploration had been introduced at this early stage of treatment, the focus remained on allowing the youngster to experiment with and develop his own style of self-expression.

Figure 1

Over the next few months, Cliff created the two sculptures represented in Figures 2 and 3. Both were important to Cliff and he invested
a great deal of time and energy in their completion. Figure 2, an open-
mouthed clay frog, can be understood as a sublimated expression of the
dependent longings that Cliff experienced in relation to maternal figures.
The gaping mouth is passively demanding and Cliff characterized it as
"unfillable." Figure 3 represents the other side of Cliff's struggles; the
aggressive impulses which overwhelmed and often stimulated him. Putting
a gold chain leash around the Plasticine dragon's neck, Cliff described
the beast as "otherwise uncontrollable." On the surface, this dragon and
the fire coming out of its open mouth are the antithesis of the impoverished frog. Yet these two symbols merely represent opposing sides of
the anguished internal battle experienced by their creator. In tandem
they can be understood as an expression of the age-typical polarization
between frightening longings for attachment and equally anxiety-provoking aggressive efforts at separation.

It was becoming important for the art therapist to channel Cliff's
creative productivity to facilitate treatment goals. Consequently, loosely
structured attempts were made to help Cliff delineate the expression of
his struggles in a way that would be beneficial to him. Both art therapy
directives and media selection were considered in the effort to provide
the youngster with material for self-exploration. Attempting to lead Cliff
to an eventual understanding of the relationship among his feared impulses, his reactive defenses and his consequent behavior, the art therapist
conceptualized a directive that differentiated feelings, fantasies and behaviors. Figure 4 is the collage Cliff produced in response.

On the left side of Figure 4, Cliff accurately depicted his fears of
aggressive and consuming impulses in his selection of the open-mouthed
hippopotamus. Not unlike the frog and the turtle, this beast cries out
aggressively for nurturance. In the center of the collage, Cliff portrayed
his sense of the "two-dimensional" person he must become in order to
control his feelings. The picture of the cardboard person poignantly
suggests the energy depletion and consequent depersonalization common
in highly defended adolescents. Cliff translated the third part of the
directive into an expression of his wishes for the future, selecting a
picture of an eagle in flight to portray his hope for freedom from
conflicts.

The collage in Figure 4 illustrates Cliff's capacity to move from
spontaneous art projects to directed tasks that demand self-exploration.

Figure 2

Figure 3

I wish _____

I am _____

I Fear _____
Monster

Figure 4

The artwork made apparent the fact that Cliff would be able to harness his talent and creativity for psychotherapeutic exploration. However, because of the tremendous power in Cliff's undirected efforts, treatment was to become, for the art therapist, a delicate balance between facilitating and directing self-expression.

Cliff remained eager to draw throughout all of his participation in art therapy. Figure 5 is one example of a series of boat drawings on which he worked for several months. Most of the drawings from this series included stormy seas and almost all depicted isolated vessels far from land. Figure 5, titled "Ship in Boatyard," is an interesting departure from the theme. Significantly, it was created after a discussion he had with the art therapist about the self-representative qualities in all the boat drawings. In this drawing the boat is contained within a protective fence, separated from the stormy sea still visible at the top of the page. Cliff was able to acknowledge the symbolic significance of this picture as he discussed his understanding that the ship needed to retreat from the storm and find a safe place where it could receive corrective help. Cliff was most certainly referring, within the metaphor, to the containment and encouragement he was experiencing at the treatment agency. For the first time in art therapy he was able to tolerate a direct interpretation of a drawing and the art therapist continued her remarks about the boat's resemblance to his own situation. Cliff had already made tremendous progress from the youngster who had originally attempted to "consume" all the art materials in the room.

In retrospect, Figure 5 appears to represent a milestone in Cliff's treatment, a point at which he began to understand the value that the art expression could play in his therapeutic progress. From this point on, his art productions tended to focus on treatment issues and he became increasingly capable of harnessing, on his own, his powerful creativity.

Figure 6 is a pencil drawing that signals a major shift in style that Cliff made as treatment progressed. No longer wanting to draw completed and preorganized pictures, Cliff began a series of simply drawn sketches embellished with images that directly illustrated his ongoing verbal associations. During this stage of treatment, the art therapist's remarks and questions helped Cliff sustain the opening-up process the artwork itself was facilitating. As Cliff became more adept at using his drawing ability to communicate his internal process, his artwork began to look more fragmented. Although this stylistic change may appear regressive,

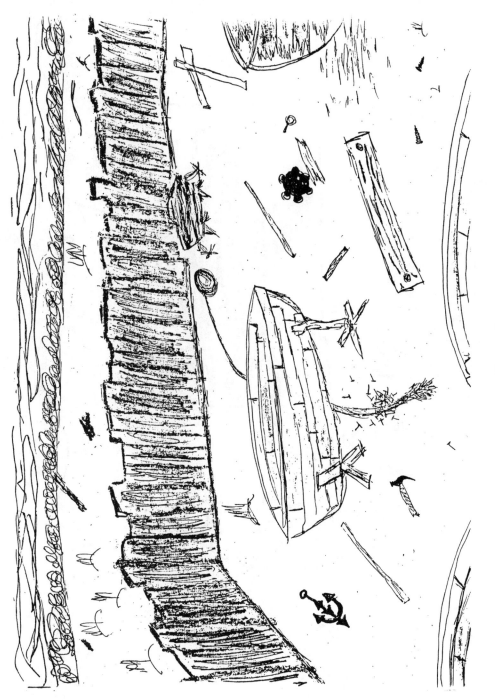

Figure 5

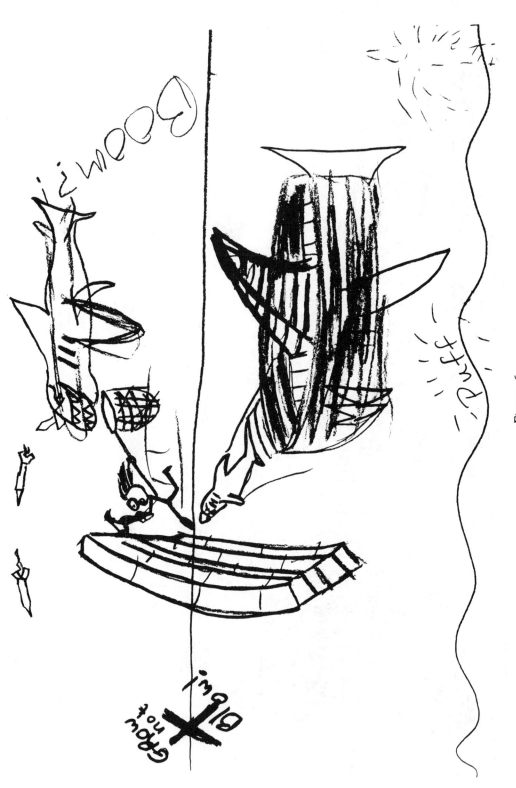

Figure 6

the increasing availability of primary process material was an important step for this adolescent whose intrapsychic struggles had previously only been acted out. In Figure 6 Cliff depicted his fears that the boat, an accepted self-representation, could easily transform itself into a shark, another open-mouthed beast. As Cliff discussed his work with the art therapist and shared his verbal associations to the imagery, he continued drawing. The final piece illustrates the boy's dawning consciousness of his own responsibility in working toward emotional equilibrium. Cliff's introduction of the phrase "Grow, not Blow!" and its implied hope that the youngster would grow to understand and find alternatives to his impulsive behavior spelled out the direction of the remainder of his treatment.

Sensing that treatment had reached an important plateau, the art therapist attempted to help Cliff explore his behavior by probing a little deeper into his repressed impulses. Reacting to this untimely intervention, Cliff used his graphic expression (Figure 7) to communicate his need to postpone the acknowledged next step.

Cliff began this marker drawing with the central image of a capital letter "F," embellished with a frightened-looking face and the rest of the word "fear." When asked about his "fear," Cliff drew the two figures on the right side of the page. The top image is reminiscent of his open-mouthed beasts and its message "I have not yet begun to think!" suggests Cliff's awareness of (but unpreparedness for) the requirements for continued progress. The lower image represents Cliff's sustained defenses around the repressed material symbolized throughout his treatment by the "box." Cliff understood and expressed through the metaphor the idea that in order to "close the mouth" he must "open the box," a step for which he was apparently still not ready.

Although Figure 7 appears to express Cliff's resistances to therapeutic intervention, it is in fact a statement of much greater optimism. In this drawing the adolescent has been able to articulate his fears and begin to understand their basis, a very important step before mastery of those fears can occur.

The marker drawing in Figure 8 is a graphic reflection of the precarious emotional state in which Cliff found himself at this midway point in art therapy treatment. The creature that the youngster selected for self-representation in this drawing has a dramatically closed mouth (reflecting Cliff's increasing control of impulsive behavior) but is tentatively perched, surrounded by landscape sketched with anxious and

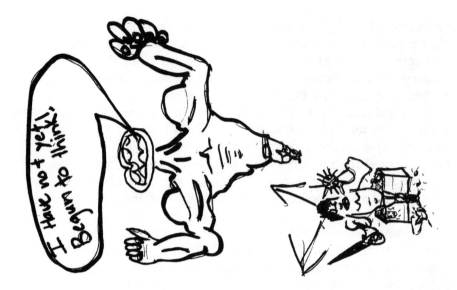

Figure 7

Figure 8

agitated lines. Cliff selected words from the collage box to create a title for this drawing, a technique he would use over and over again, as he attempted to understand the meanings of his drawings. The title of Figure 8, "Who Can Wait A Life Away," suggests Cliff's understanding of the imperative need to continue his progress in therapy. Cliff remained at this treatment plateau for several weeks, struggling with the conflicting defensive and progressive pulls. The art therapist remained encouraging but respectful during this agonizing process as the adolescent integrated his previous gains in preparation for the final stage of treatment.

In order to structure the expressive risks he now had to take, Cliff expanded his use of a symbol that he had introduced earlier. The "box," symbolizing unacknowledged feelings and intrapsychic material, became an important element in most of Cliff's drawings from this point on. In the marker drawing in Figure 9, the box is held by a (this time almost "mouthless") creature whose thoughts show his concern about becoming robotlike if he is unable to open the "box." It was clear to both Cliff and the art therapist that the "box" was a metaphorical expression of his most internalized secrets. It was also clear that Cliff would need help finding a structured and anxiety-minimizing method for opening and exploring the contents.

For the next several months Cliff continued to draw the human/monster figure he had introduced in Figure 9. As he developed this series he began to discuss the episodes in which he had molested his half-sisters. He also initiated discussion about his feelings toward his mother and her husband. Although Cliff created no drawings that directly reflected the content of the verbalized material, he did produce many that provided signposts in Cliff's route toward an increasingly stable ego. Figure 10, which portrays Cliff's deep shame over his uncontrolled impulses, is such a drawing.

Many symbols appear in this important drawing. In the center Cliff included the increasingly humanized self-representative figure. His/its portrayal as one-legged, shark-armed and cut off at the neck suggests Cliff's continuing struggles with his wounded self-image and his continuing preoccupation with impulses. The partly opened tin can just to the left of the figure's left knee is this drawing's version of the "box." In this picture, the "box" has begun to open and Cliff acknowledges that the "Polaroide" image he has of himself has consequently become a facade and his "footprints" (i.e., behavior for which he is remembered) give his real nature away. Clearly, Cliff has begun to deal with the material

Figure 9

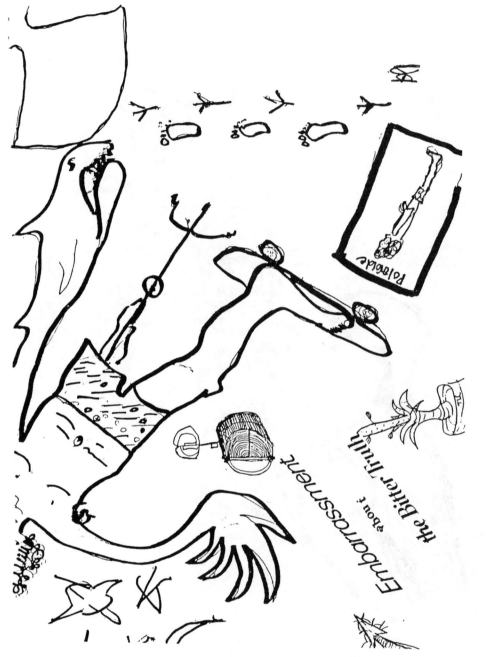

Embarrassment about the Bitter Truth

Figure 10

he has repressed for so long. It is not easy and Cliff needs much support throughout the process. However, his title for this picture, "Embarrassment about the Bitter Truth," indicates his therapeutic gains. Cliff's embarrassment and more importantly his ability to communicate his embarrassment suggest the increasing strength of his superego as he began to develop healthier intrapsychic structure.

Figure 11 was drawn in response to the art therapist's encouragement to create the box he had first depicted in Figure 9. In this version Cliff placed the self-representative figure within the box, appearing trapped between three imploding hydraulic forces that are closing in on him. Cliff labeled the spiked ball to which the figure is chained as "Therapy," an expression of his feelings that although treatment provided him with a potential tool to break out of the glass box, it also prevented him from escaping the pressure of the forces. Therapy had become a lifeline for Cliff but as his self-exploration continued, his anxiety over disclosures remained high.

Owing to Cliff's overall improvement termination from the agency was imminent and the focus of art therapy treatment changed to an effort to consolidate Cliff's enormous gains. In the course of a final four weeks, several drawings were created. Only one, Figure 12, is included to represent the work of termination.

Figure 12 was Cliff's graphic response to the art therapist's encouragement to depict the course of his treatment. In this drawing, Cliff was able to express his sense of his own progress. He firmly asserted his belief that "self-expression" had been the key in his treatment. He symbolized "Therapy" with fuel pumps along the road, refilling him with "new ideas." Although his inclusion of a sphinx, which he titled "The Riddle," suggests his acknowledgment of many unanswered questions, his hopeful message comes across clearly.

It is no more possible to tell where the path in this picture leads than to predict Cliff's own future. However, the therapeutic gains he achieved through the emphasis on self-expression in the art therapy modality are significant. An impulse-ridden adolescent in the beginning of treatment, Cliff terminated as a more mature, self-aware and self-monitoring young adult. Art therapy had helped Cliff achieve and consolidate the developmental gains that his early history had impeded.

Cliff's art therapy treatment can best be understood as a series of steps from defensively motivated impulsive behavior to the discovery of an alternative modality of expression as an outlet for the same intrapsychic

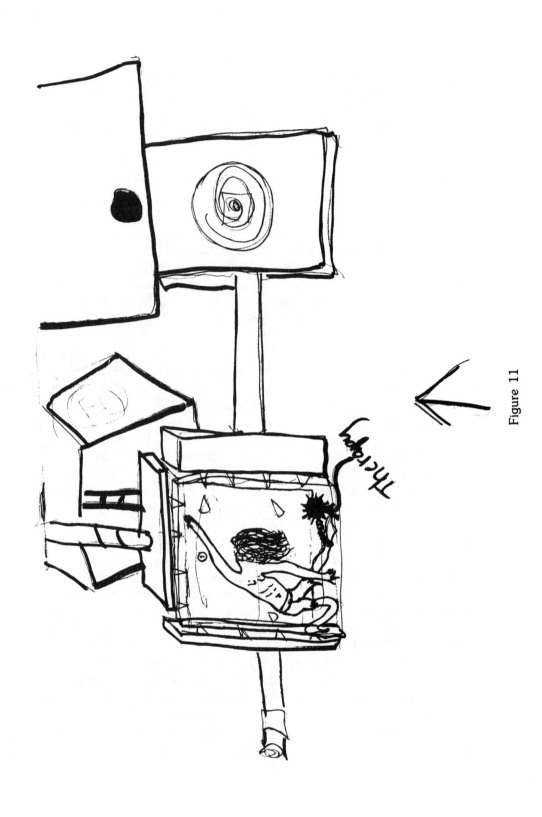

Figure 11

Figure 12

material. Cliff began art therapy interested only in "consuming" the art materials. As his productions provided expression for his internal conflicts with increasing clarity, he was helped to explore the meaning of these communications. As he began to feel more comfortable with the graphic expression of his internal conflicts he was able to use this modality to share the repressed material at the core of his conflicts. His treatment had taken many months but the patience and encouragement of the art therapist had allowed this troubled adolescent to evolve his own style of expression according to his own intrapsychic timetable.

CASE 2: SUZANNE

The second case discussed in this chapter is very different from the first. It involves the art therapy treatment of a severely disturbed adolescent experiencing frequent episodes of active psychosis. The case material and therapeutic interventions are carefully analyzed in order to contrast art therapy approaches with these two very different types of adolescents.

Suzanne was a fifteen-year-old girl, diagnosed as schizophrenic, childhood type, who had been living at the agency where treatment occurred for two years prior to her referral for art therapy. Before placement she had lived through many traumatic experiences including extreme infantalization, sexual abuse and parental deprivation. Although she had progressed a great deal during her two years at the facility and had formed strong attachments to several members of the treatment team, she continued to present herself as frail and helpless, frequently dealing with her anxiety by retreating into an infantile, psychotic state. She was referred to art therapy in the hope of helping her achieve age-appropriate self-expression.

Initially Suzanne found the new relationship and the new modality of art therapy threatening and she remained silent during the first few sessions. Rather than encouraging her to talk, the art therapist made a variety of art supplies available for her self-expression. Suzanne appeared to find the art process a welcome relief from the anxiety generated by this new encounter and eagerly selected drawing paper and crayons. Throughout her first few sessions she created a series of drawings, each of which depicted a nursery full of babies. Figure 13 is representative of this series.

The "nursery" described in all of Suzanne's early drawings was very real to this adolescent, as were all of the individual babies that she

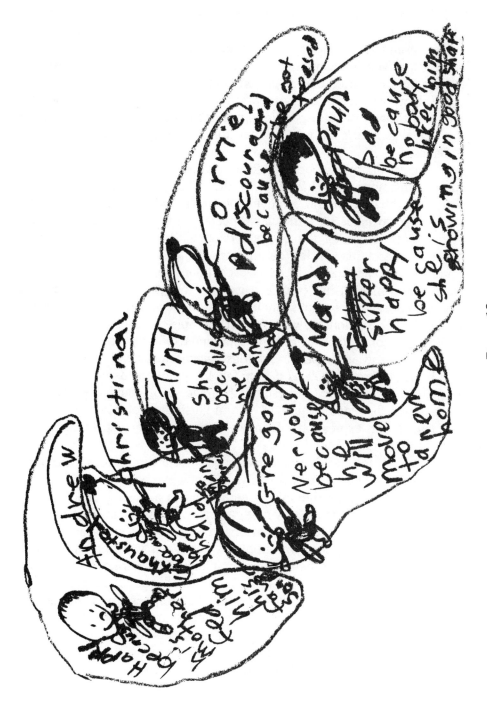

Figure 13

included. Although the infants and their feelings were clearly projections of Suzanne's own internal experiences, her capacity to acknowledge the self-representative symbolism was severely limited by her impaired ego functioning. The conglomerate of babies was indeed a personal expression for Suzanne, distorted and displaced because of her severe psychopathology. However, for Suzanne to progress emotionally, it was important for the art therapist to respect (and not debilitate through interpretation) the valuable treatment vehicle that this "nursery" metaphor was to provide.

The art therapist concentrated on promoting Suzanne's attempts to share something about her inner world. After several sessions of perseverated drawing of the same infants over and over again, Suzanne was helped to focus on particular aspects of the complicated metaphor at one time. Since all the babies looked alike and for the most part failed to reflect the written descriptions of feelings assigned to them, Suzanne was encouraged to draw each infant separately, discussing its feelings and making her own face express the given emotion. Suzanne worked for several sessions on this task of developing her expressive range. As her relationship with the art therapist progressed and she felt increasingly comfortable with the questioning exploration of her drawings, her pictures and accompanying stories became fuller and more detailed. The babies began to look as if they felt the emotions assigned to them, and Suzanne began to understand that she, too, could express these feelings with her face. Figure 14 is one illustration of Suzanne's efforts at refining her expression of anger, metaphorically expressed in the persona of infant "Paul."

Although the decision had been made not to point out to Suzanne, at this early point in treatment, the obvious symbolic function of her baby drawings, the art therapist once alluded to a possible link between the drawings and Suzanne's own experiences. Knowing she had recently been rewarded for improved behavior in her cottage, the therapist asked Suzanne to compare her own happiness about this with the happy baby she drew in her next art therapy session. Figure 15 illustrates her reaction.

Suzanne began the drawing with the small pair of figures slightly left of center that are labeled with her "scared" response to the therapist's "mean" probing of her feelings. She quickly added the title, "What makes me happy?," across the top of the page—both restating the art therapist's question and indicating her understanding that her feelings were the issue. Reacting defensively to this threatening demand, she

Figure 14

then retreated into yet another reworking of the original "nursery" theme, denying the negative feelings expressed initially in this drawing. Clearly she was not ready to confront her feelings, to give up the metaphor she still required for communication. Her subtle manipulation of the metaphor had itself made that point. Suzanne resisted the confrontation of the art therapist by regressing to an earlier drawing style. Once again the babies' expressions and their assigned emotions are limited. Overall, Figure 15 depicts a defensive retreat from the richer communication she had accomplished earlier. It was apparent that Suzanne's need for disguised expression had to be allowed to evolve at its own pace.

101

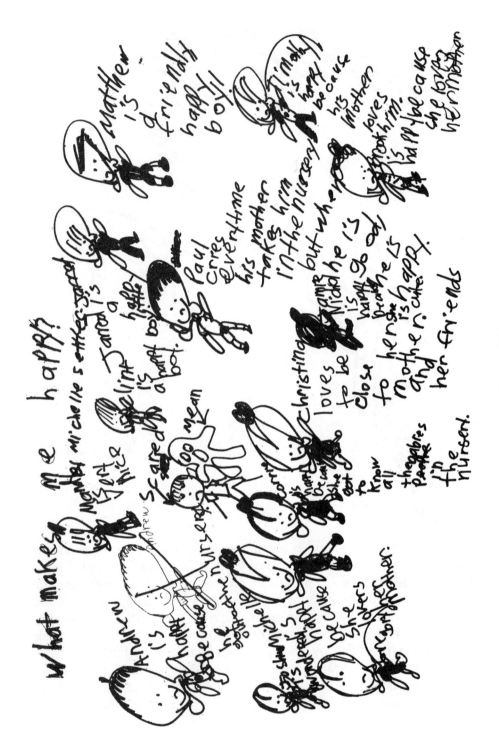

Figure 15

In her fourth month of art therapy Suzanne suddenly stopped creating baby drawings and began sorting through the magazine pictures that had been placed in the collage box. She spent several sessions selecting all of the baby pictures and then proceeded to create collages using each of her selections separately. Figure 16 is typical of her early work in this medium.

Like Suzanne's other collages, Figure 16 focuses on the theme of maternal caretaking, hinting perhaps at her transference feelings. Although she maintained her metaphorical use of baby pictures for self-expression, no longer did each baby stand alone simply as a projection of a feeling. Rather the babies became participants in relationships, relationships that echoed—with corrective, more nurturing adaptations—Suzanne's own early experiences. Positioning her (still disguised) self-representations in the context of a family system was clearly a sign of expressive progress for Suzanne.

The switch from drawing to collage was accompanied by several changes in Suzanne's behavior during the sessions. She perseverated less and sustained eye contact with the art therapist more frequently. Her associations to her artwork became richer, perhaps because the realism of the photographic images stimulated her. The fact that the collage process provided Suzanne with a more intimate means of expression than her own rudimentary use of the actual artistic process suggests her dependence on externally imposed boundaries for self-expression. With an adolescent as severely damaged as Suzanne, the primary process potential in open-ended artistic expression can become an obstacle in the development of integrated expression.

A few weeks after the completion of Figure 16, Suzanne created the collage in Figure 17, illustrating a more developed use of the collage technique. Delighting in the stories she could create around the baby pictures, Suzanne originated a practice she called "putting words into peoples' mouths." The family in Figure 17 can be understood as capable of filling Suzanne's wish for the kind of infancy she never had. In this expression of Suzanne's fantasy, the nurturing mother is not only attentive to the baby's needs ("oh, you need to be changed") but also protective ("Karen, you can't hold her . . ."). The father, unlike Suzanne's own sexually abusive father, is passive and unintrusive.

At this point in treatment Suzanne appeared to be on the verge of acknowledging that the babies represented her. Occasionally she unthinkingly substituted the pronoun "I" for the pronoun "she" in talking about

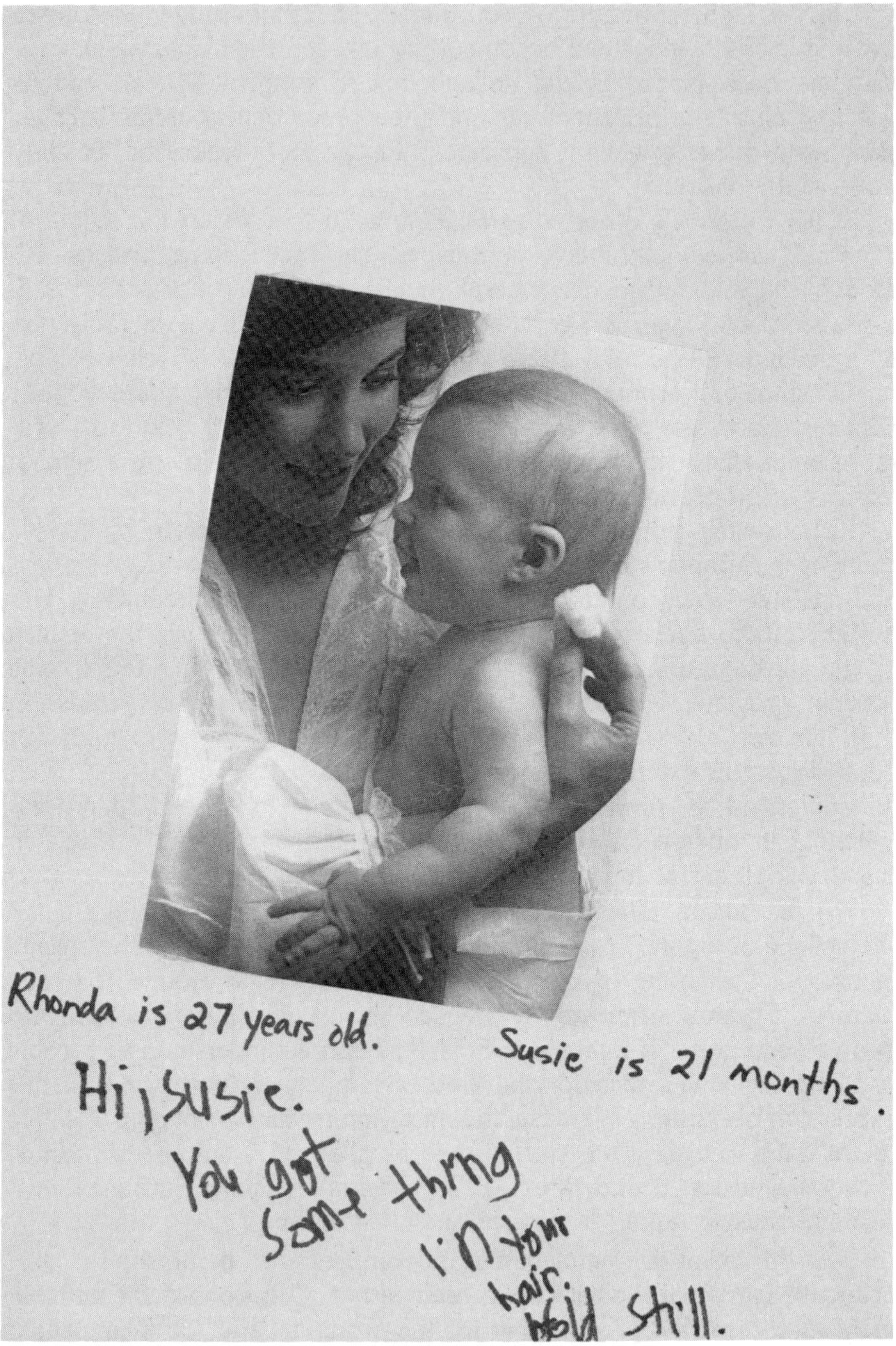

Rhonda is 27 years old.   Susie is 21 months.

Hi, Susie.
You got
some thing
in your
hair.
hold still.

Figure 16

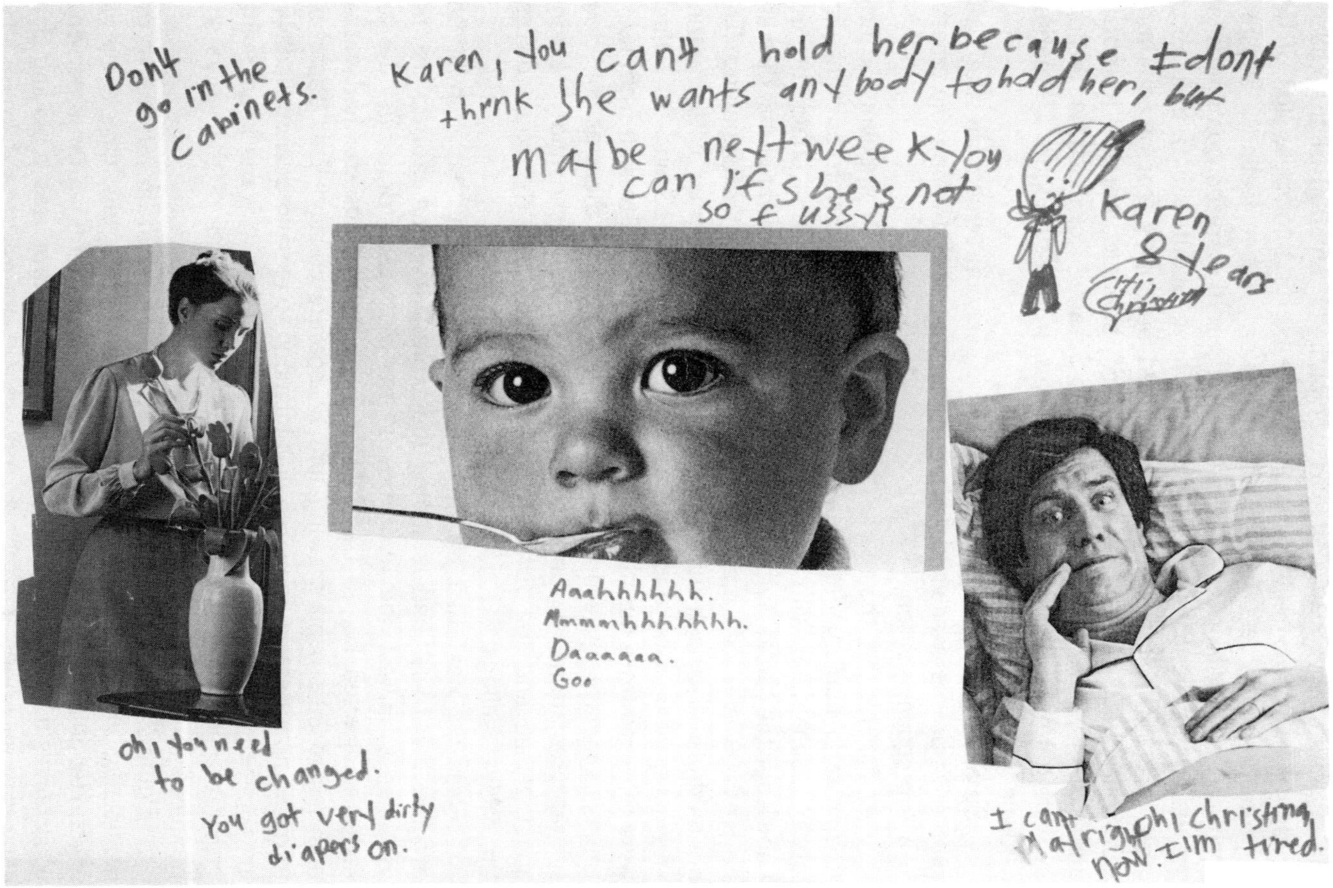

Don't go in the cabinets.

oh you need to be changed. You got very dirty diapers on.

Karen, you can't hold her because I dont think she wants anybody to hold her, but maybe next week K-Joy can it's she's not so fussy.

Karen 8 years Chicago

Aahhhhh.
Mmmmhhhhhh.
Daaaaaa.
Goo

I can't right now i'm tired. Maybe right now i'm tired. now

Figure 17

the babies in her collages. It was not until the creation of the collage in Figure 18, however, that Suzanne gave the first concrete sign of her approaching readiness for direct expression of her feelings. Suzanne produced this collage in response to the art therapist's comments on the different feelings she appeared to have about babies and about growing up. The imagery clearly reflected Suzanne's fear of adulthood and consequent clinging to infancy (and infantile fantasy) to obtain gratification. As the first artwork in which Suzanne expressed her feelings in a straightforward fashion, without resort to fantasy, Figure 18 marked a turning point in treatment.

Suzanne's progress in response to encouragement in the self-expressive process was validated by the unprompted drawing she created in a subsequent session.

At first glance, the marker drawing in Figure 19 appears identical to her early nursery drawings. However, in this version Suzanne has labeled each infant with *her own name*. That Suzanne could thus acknowledge the babies' self-representational function indicated that disguise no longer was as desperately necessary to her as in the beginning. The art therapist discussed this new version of her metaphor with Suzanne at length, comparing and contrasting it to Figures 13 and 14, which were retrieved from her file. Recognizing her own progression from using babies as fantasy projections of her feelings to using them as conscious self-representations, Suzanne spoke of the difficulty she had in talking about herself and the comparative ease with which she could discuss the babies' feelings.

Over the next two months, Suzanne took a further step in her progress toward self-understanding and expression. In an effort to channel the intense interest she now took in her very early drawings, the art therapist directed her to translate each of the feelings she had earlier represented in a baby drawing into a separate collage. This departure from the nondirective approach was intended to expand Suzanne's dawning capacity to link the projections in her drawings with the inner reality they represented. The collage in Figure 20 is typical of the works she produced in response to this directive.

Figure 20 demonstrates Suzanne's expression of an interactive dynamic that was linked to an earlier baby drawing involving a simple affect. Her ability to relate the projected affective states with interpersonal occurrences marked Suzanne's progress. Art therapy was providing Suzanne with an opportunity to expand her self-expression and explore the

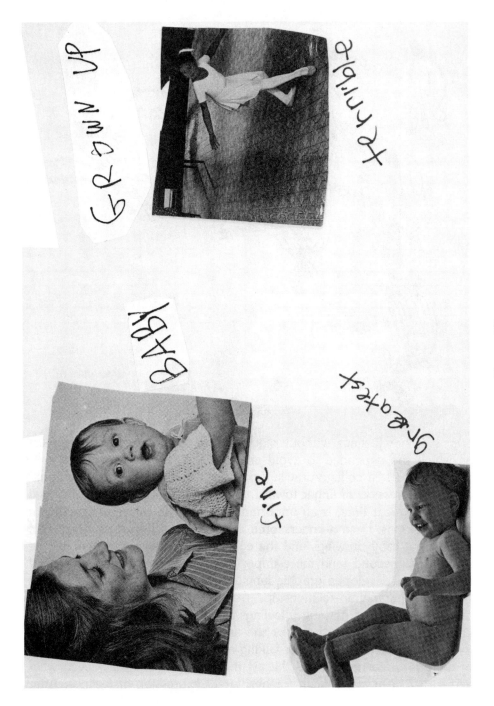

GROWN UP

terrible

BABY

greatest

fine

Figure 18

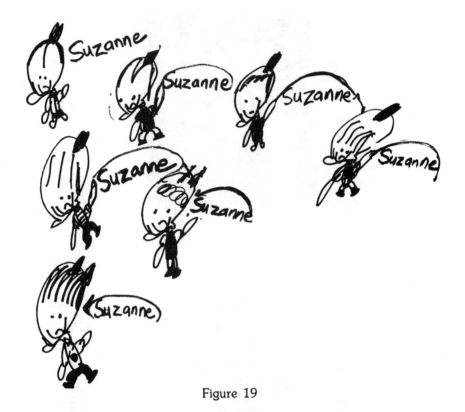

Figure 19

origins of her feelings without requiring her to give up the maneuvers on which she depended to avoid anxiety.

Figure 21, a collage/drawing executed shortly thereafter as a spontaneous expression of anger toward the art therapist for having changed her appointment time, is an important milestone in Suzanne's treatment for two reasons. First, it underscored the identical self-expressive function of both the baby drawings and the collages by juxtaposing them on the same page. Second (and more important), it involved Suzanne's use of her now well-developed graphic language to express immediate feelings about the therapeutic relationship. In this production Suzanne used art materials to express her angry feelings in both forms of her metaphorical language. As in her early works she assigned an alias ("Janel") to her two self-representations, but in talking about the picture, Suzanne spoke of her angry feelings toward the art therapist. Thus she achieved what had earlier been too difficult for her: direct expression of feelings. After

108

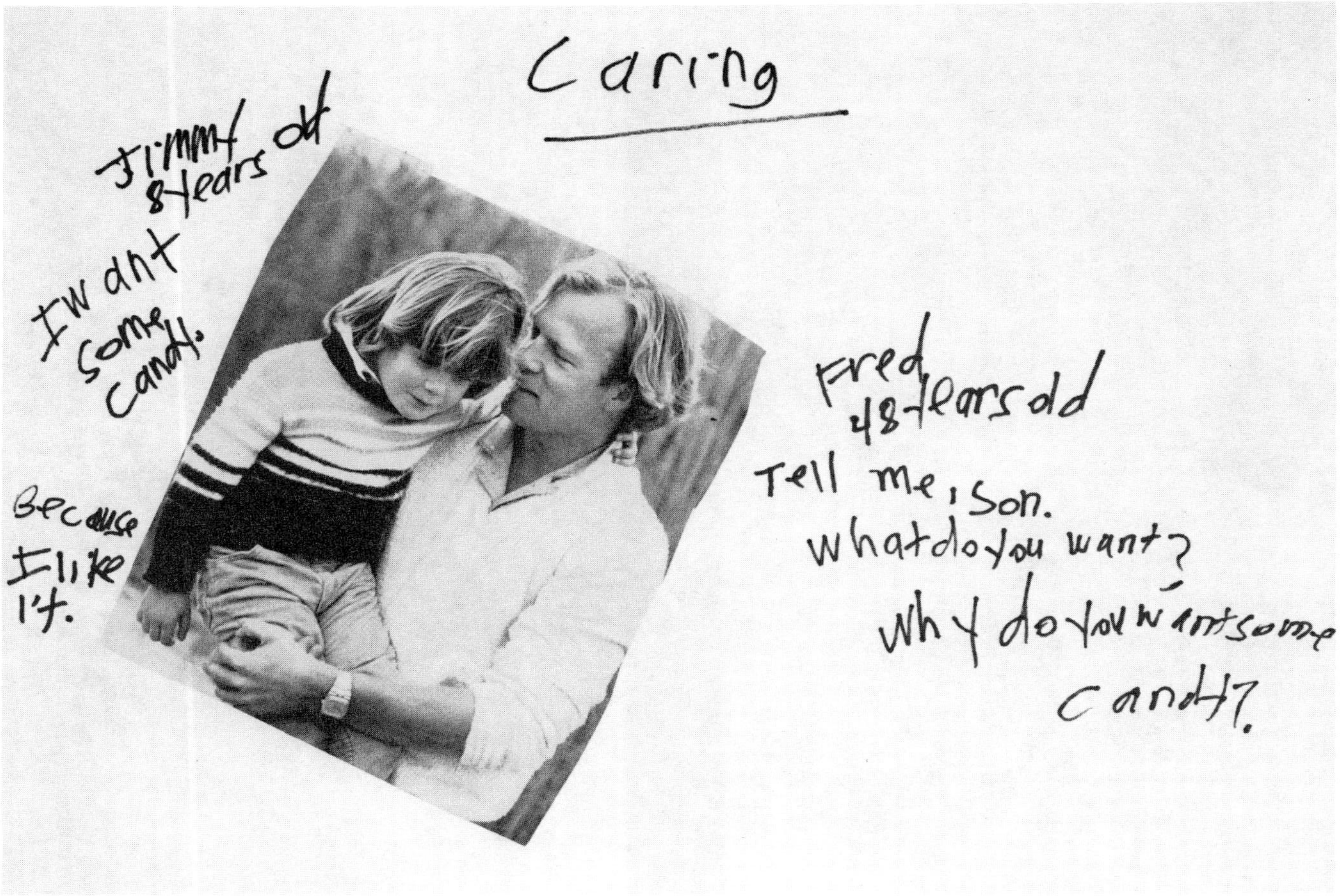

Caring
Jimmy 8 years old
I want some candy.
Because I like it.
Fred 48 years old
Tell me, son.
What do you want?
Why do you want some candy?

Figure 20

Figure 21

projecting her anger onto the paper by means of both drawing and collage, she was able to acknowledge it in speech.

Suzanne's lengthy experimentation with disguised self-revelation had gradually led to increasingly direct disclosures. The use of art materials had provided her with a new means of communication, which in turn had helped her establish a relationship with the art therapist. That relationship, however, had to be terminated prematurely because of the therapist's departure from the treatment center. Knowing that the relationship had become important to Suzanne, the art therapist realized that Suzanne would need help to express her feelings about its approaching end. It was hoped that Suzanne would be able to make use of the self-expressive skills she had developed in art therapy to explore the upcoming separation.

Figure 22 depicts Suzanne's responses to the art therapist's encouragement to delineate the changes she had experienced in her feelings over the course of the treatment relationship. Suzanne began on the left side, representing her initial fears with one of her stereotypic renderings of a baby that accurately recalled her earliest artwork, in which she labeled babies to match her own feelings. In the center of the paper, Suzanne drew a flowing scribble to represent her more relaxed feelings after several months of art therapy. This middle phase of treatment she assigned to the period when she produced the self-expressive collages. On the far right Suzanne exercised the self-expressive voice she had developed over the course of treatment to speak by word and shape of her anxiety over the impending separation. It is astounding how accurately this recapitulation of Suzanne's modes of graphic expression summarized her therapeutic progress.

Just before leaving the session in which Figure 22 was created, Suzanne turned the page over and drew a tearful baby on the back, adding the words "mad" and "angry" (Figure 22a). This spontaneous addition to her drawing documents the regression Suzanne experienced during the termination of art therapy. Returning to her early defensive drawing style was the only way that this adolescent felt safe enough to express her feelings over the upcoming separation. It is important to point out that this regression, typical of the terminating phase of treatment, did not negate the progress Suzanne had made, but rather further substantiated her developing capacity to understand and make use of an increasingly large repertoire of expressive styles.

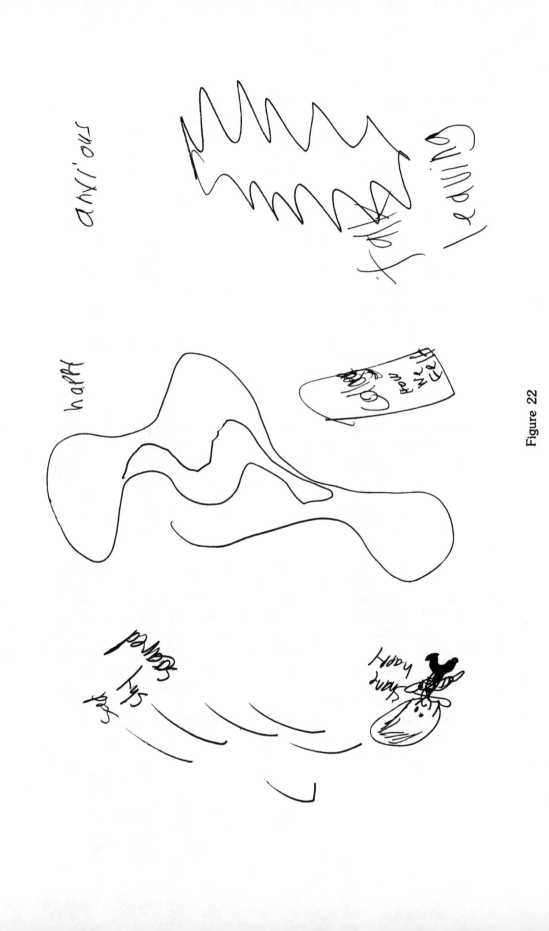

Figure 22

Figure 22a

Suzanne had been in art therapy for only nine months, but her response to both the use of art materials and the therapeutic relationship was positive. Suzanne discovered in the art process a new mode of communication that helped her establish a relationship with another person. As her trust and comfort in that relationship grew, she began to take risks with self-exposure, bringing her previously internal world out into the open. The early, heavily disguised works were eventually replaced by increasingly self-representational products. As treatment progressed, Suzanne was able to use the art materials for communication of feelings that could be understood even without verbal explanation.

COMPARISON OF THE TWO CASES

This case material illustrates two very different kinds of adolescent psychopathology as well as two very different approaches to art therapy treatment. In the first case, Cliff presented with acting-out behavioral

113

symptoms, typical of the adolescent repressing internal conflicts. In the second case, the much weaker ego of the more disturbed adolescent was not capable of that kind of defensive maneuver, and instead allowed for retreat into a psychotic state. Both adolescents can be understood as responding to the tremendous amounts of anxiety generated by the developmental demands of separation and autonomy and exacerbated by problematic early development. However, because of the difference in the timing and severity of the abandonments and confusions, Suzanne's defensive responses (psychosis) caused much greater dysfunction than Cliff's (conduct disorder).

In response to the very different presentations of these two adolescents, art therapy approaches were conceived very differently for each. Cliff was encouraged to expand his spontaneous expression and to channel his productions toward self-exploration. Directives became increasingly explicit and challenging as treatment progressed and Cliff was guided toward the acquisition of insight about his behavioral/artistic expressions. In a very different approach Suzanne was helped to experiment with her defensive patterns of expression with the hope of making her feelings increasingly available for acknowledgment. Directives were, for the most part, less challenging and more open-ended. Insight was not a goal with Suzanne and treatment focused on helping this isolated adolescent develop an ability to share internal experiences.

These two cases have been contrasted in an effort to illustrate the spectrum of approaches that can be taken within the art therapy modality. Since adolescence is a developmental stage in which creativity and artistic expression are paramount, the art process can be harnessed for psychotherapeutic growth with the entire spectrum of psychopathology. It is important, however, that the art therapist understand and conceive treatment goals and approaches with a sensitivity to the particular dynamics of each adolescent client.

5

Adjunctive Art Therapy

In residential treatment centers and inpatient facilities for adolescents, youngsters encounter many helping professionals. Very often, the art therapist is one among many mental health workers with whom the adolescent patient may develop a relationship. It is important for the art therapist to understand his/her role in relation to the treatment team before establishing a therapeutic approach. This chapter defines an adjunctive role that the art therapist can very successfully play in conjunction with the other professionals on the team. In this role, working along with social workers, psychologists and psychiatrists to further the psychotherapeutic growth of the adolescent patient, the art therapist can most beneficially provide the valuable self-expressive opportunities inherent in the art modality.

Material in this chapter is adapted from Greenspoon, D. The Role of the Art Therapist as an Adjunctive Member of a Residential Treatment Team. *Residential Group Care and Treatment,* 2(3), 1984, by permission of Haworth Press.

To maximize the therapeutic potential of the art modality, the art therapist must be sensitive to his/her orientation among his/her co-workers. Lack of clarity regarding the relationship between adjunctive and primary therapists is detrimental to the adolescents' therapeutic progress. The model described in this chapter is based on the understanding that the most significant difference between primary and adjunctive therapy lies in the area of the therapist's response to transference material. A case example illustrates how adjunctive therapy can help adolescents explore difficult feelings which originated in earlier relationships without making the connections between these feelings and their antecedents. In this model, art therapy functions as a facilitator of expression to catalyze the insights that will be fully explored in the primary therapy.

In an agency which utilizes the treatment team approach, there are, in a variety of roles, many adults interacting with the adolescents who have been separated from their families. Mayer (1960), writing about residential treatment, acknowledges that all members of the staff of a treatment facility become parental substitutes. He divides the staff into three categories based on their substitutional roles: the power parents (administrators), the care parents (child care workers) and the transference parents (therapists). Addressing the fact that youngsters placed in residential treatment are likely to respond to the staff in ways that repeat their relationships with their actual parents, Mayer differentiates the staff categories partly in terms of recommended responses to these transference reactions. He says:

> An institution which is full of adults offers many opportunities
> to the child for such a transfer of these unreasonable, inap-
> propriate feelings . . . it is only the therapist who can permit
> the transference. (p. 283)

Traditionally, in residential treatment centers and inpatient adolescent units, the role of the transference-permitting psychotherapist is filled by psychiatric social workers. The care parents (child care workers and recreational therapists) are encouraged to provide consistent and corrective responses to the children's interactions, not to analyze or explore them. In this way the psychotherapists are significantly differentiated from the milieu therapists. The category of adjunctive therapy (as established in this model) seems to straddle the definitions of both psy-

116

chotherapy and milieu therapy and needs to be fully defined. It is accurate but simplistic to explain the role of the adjunctive clinical art therapist as a facilitator of the release and expression of affective material through the use of spontaneous artwork. Defined in this manner the art therapist's role has a milieu orientation that contradicts its essentially psychotherapeutic orientation. This definition is inadequate because it disregards the transference reactions accompanying a relationship that tolerates the regression, aggression and conflicts that inevitably surface in art productions. The unanswered question remains the manner in which the transference reactions in the art therapy relationship are handled. The literature on residential treatment is of little help. Frequently adjunctive therapists are described as primarily offering recreational services and the psychotherapeutic aspect of the adjunct role is minimized. Evangelakis (1974) exemplifies this position in the following statement:

> Aiding the physical development of the children, building their confidence, training them in social values, reaching their education and utilizing these experiences as therapy for their emotional problems are all part of the adjunctive therapies service. (p. 104)

From a different perspective, Kramer (1958), an art therapist for many years at the Wiltwyck School for Boys, also separates the adjunctive art therapy from the youngsters' psychotherapy:

> Through their painting the children learn to know themselves better. They become acquainted with their likes and dislikes, and as they develop an individual style of painting, they learn to understand and accept themselves. (p. 125)

When the art therapist is understood as a recreation therapist (Evangelakis, 1974) or as a facilitator of the inherently therapeutic quality of the art process (Kramer, 1958), the psychotherapeutic issue of transference is not addressed. In the model presented in this chapter, the adjunctive therapist functions psychotherapeutically, that is, fully acknowledging transference material. While avoiding conflictual treatment issues with other members of the treatment team, and fully utilizing the art modality, he/she is able to participate in the psychodynamic aspects of the adolescent's treatment.

117

A treatment team approach with adolescents is often complex and sometimes problematic. Since art therapy can have a significant impact with youngsters in this stage of development it is important that an art therapy approach that is easily integrated into the treatment team be developed. Art therapy can function in many ways, but its role as a facilitator of self-expression, complementary to the work of primary therapy, must not be oversimplified. The adjunctive art therapist faces many difficulties and complexities that can be minimized with role clarification.

The remainder of this chapter explores the case of a fifteen-year-old patient in a residential treatment center to illustrate the adjunctive role that art therapy can play when conceptualized as a support for the goals of an entire treatment team. Seen in primary therapy by a social worker, for medication assessment by a psychiatrist and for diagnostic evaluation by a psychologist, he was referred for adjunctive therapy with the art therapist. Art therapy was to become a very significant element in this boy's overall treatment, but it must be understood in the context of all the other therapeutic experiences he was undergoing.

The role of the adjunctive therapist is defined here as the case material is explored. The American Association for Children's Residential Centers' 1972 task force's definition of the role of the psychotherapist is utilized as a basis. After the case material is examined, this definition is modified to provide a theoretical model for the role of the adjunctive art therapist within a treatment team. The unmodified definition reads as follows:

> Psychotherapist must set up communications, win trust, understand bizarre symbolic language, assess and respond to odd and perverse relationship gestures and interpret the inevitable transfer of the child's early distorted and painful relationships onto the interaction of therapist–patient. (Bettelheim, de Vryer, Mann, Norton, Noshpitz, & Pittenger, 1972, p. 13)

The adolescent discussed in this exploration of the role of the adjunctive therapist is a fifteen-year-old black boy. Luke, the youngest of eight children, was raised by his mother, who worked long hours outside the home, and by his oldest sister. His father, although able to hold a job, was an alcoholic, frequently inebriated at home. Consequently Luke's early development was characterized by role confusions and lack

118

of consistent structure. At the onset of adolescence, his early behavior problems (difficulties with impulse control) developed into full-scale delinquency as he began identifying with a street gang. Luke's upwardly mobile family attributed his problems solely to their disadvantaged neighborhood and were resistant to exploring related family issues. Luke was placed in residential treatment by the County Probation Department consequent to an accessory involvement with an attempted break and entry. Initially Luke presented himself to the treatment team as bright and charming, but manipulative and street-wise.

Prior to Luke's referral for art therapy, the social worker who was his primary therapist described his participation in psychotherapy as "performing" and "controlling." The social worker wrote:

It is possible that [Luke] avoids discussing his deeper feelings because he is genuinely confused as to what they are or even who he is.

The consulting psychologist, in his evaluative report on Luke, pointed out the underlying dynamics behind the boy's resistance to intimacy, which he manifested by entertaining and therefore distancing the psychotherapist. He wrote:

[Luke's] ego boundaries are so fragile that if he gets close to another person he begins to merge with them and not feel as if he's a separate person from them.

For the first several months of his participation in residential treatment Luke continued his superficial relationships with the staff. Treatment team members complained that he was impossible to get to know and difficult to trust. Psychotherapy seemed to be a game to him and his verbal abilities allowed him to play it well. Luke was referred to art therapy to provide him with a modality that he might experience as less threatening than verbal psychotherapy. This referral was based on the understanding that Luke's symptomatic participation in the therapy with his social worker was the result of a massive defense system. It was speculated that the adjunctive art therapy might generate less anxiety and therefore not necessitate Luke's defensive resistance. Luke was clearly not ready for verbal insight-oriented psychotherapy and it was felt that

119

adjunctive art therapy could help him past the obstacles that prevented progress with his primary psychotherapist.

Luke began participating in individual art therapy sessions with no overt resistance but he maintained an attitude of polite and controlling theatrics. The art therapist minimized her responses to this behavior and focused her efforts on encouraging Luke's spontaneous use of art materials. Luke was not a particularly talented artist and at first ridiculed suggestions to utilize the art materials. As he began to be aware of the seriousness with which the art therapist viewed art productions, he became intrigued by her suggestions. However, as his curiosity increased so did his attempts to ward off the development of any possible attachment. His ambivalence about this new therapeutic relationship surfaced quickly, manifested in his attendance patterns and in his artwork. Rather than reflecting on the etiology of this ambivalence or relating its appearance in this relationship to its antecedents in the family and in previous psychotherapeutic contacts, the art therapist responded to its graphic representation in Luke's artwork. It is this tactic that truly differentiates the adjunctive role from the primary therapy. It would have been possible at this time to interpret Luke's behavior, to point out how the intimacy of the psychotherapeutic relationship threatened him and how it related to problematic interaction within his family. Luke had not fared well with this kind of technique in the past and it appeared that the noninterpretive role of adjunctive therapy might be more successful with his defenses. Consequently, treatment remained within the metaphors that Luke created. It is important to carefully analyze the manner in which Luke's artwork was utilized in order to understand the potency of "working within the metaphor" as an important technique for the adjunctive art therapist.

Figures 1 through 4 illustrate the self-representational metaphor that Luke quickly developed in the beginning stage of his art therapy. It appears that the art therapy modality offered Luke the escape valve that his repressed need for self-expression required.

Figure 1, a spontaneously executed marker drawing, the first of a repetitive series, depicts the stage of action in which Luke would fully represent his internal struggles. In the picture, space ships attack each other as larger space stations wage aggressive war. Luke's description of the scene was confused and somewhat anxious, suggesting the affective response he had to this material. The repetition of this type of drawing,

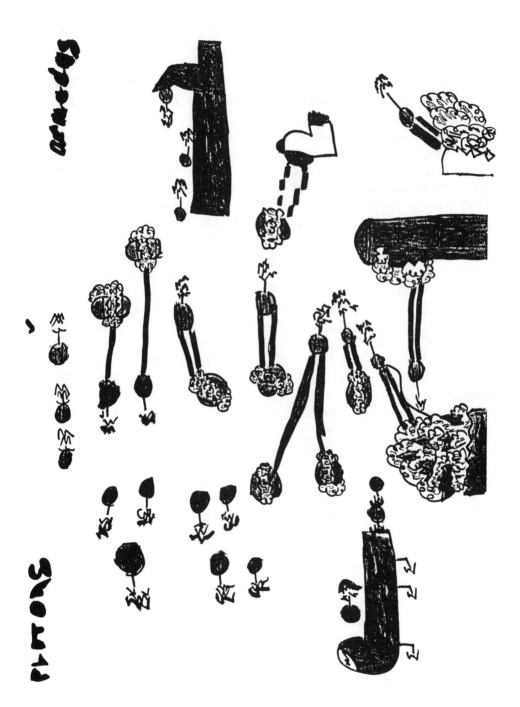

Figure 1

full of explosions, implosions, aggression and destruction, signaled its psychic significance and the art therapist responded by simply asking questions about the depicted battle.

Figure 2 was drawn in answer to the art therapist's curiosity about the origins of Luke's intergalactic war. As he was drawing, the youngster described the "expulsion" of the "attack space ship" from the "mother ship" and pointed to the planet in the upper right corner as its "destination." By focusing on one aspect of the original stage-setting drawing (i.e., the origins of the intergalactic war), the art therapist had helped Luke begin to sort out his troubling intrapsychic material. As the metaphors emerge within the art productions, it is the responsibility of the adjunctive art therapist to encourage clarity and organization.

Figure 3 was produced in response to the art therapist's interest in how the story unfolded. This technique of encouraging the chronological delineation of the metaphorical events helped Luke create an order to previously chaotic feelings. In this drawing, Luke described the attack ship as "approaching" the "target planet," but he verbalized his indecisiveness regarding the type of contact intended. He expressed his ambivalence: "it doesn't know yet, whether it will attack or be friends; it needs to check things out first." Within the metaphor, Luke was describing his own feelings regarding the psychotherapeutic intimacy of which he was so afraid. Despite the blatant underlying meanings of the art productions, the art therapist continued to work with the manifest rather than the latent material.

When asked to draw what the "contact" might look like, Luke produced Figure 4, a scene of chaos and confusion that has sent both the spaceship and the planet hurtling through space. This drawing is a poignant representation of the destructive power Luke perceives himself to have. When asked to represent contact, he lost the control which he had exhibited in his earlier drawings.

Figures 1 through 4 were selected from a lengthy series on this theme which characterized Luke's artwork for the first several months of his participation in art therapy. The four drawings can be understood as a metaphorical expression of Luke's desire for, yet fear of, intimacy. The underlying dynamic in this metaphor was the identical dynamic manifest in Luke's relationship with the agency staff, in particular with his social worker and with his art therapist. In the adjunctive art therapy, however, Luke was given the opportunity to remain within the meta-

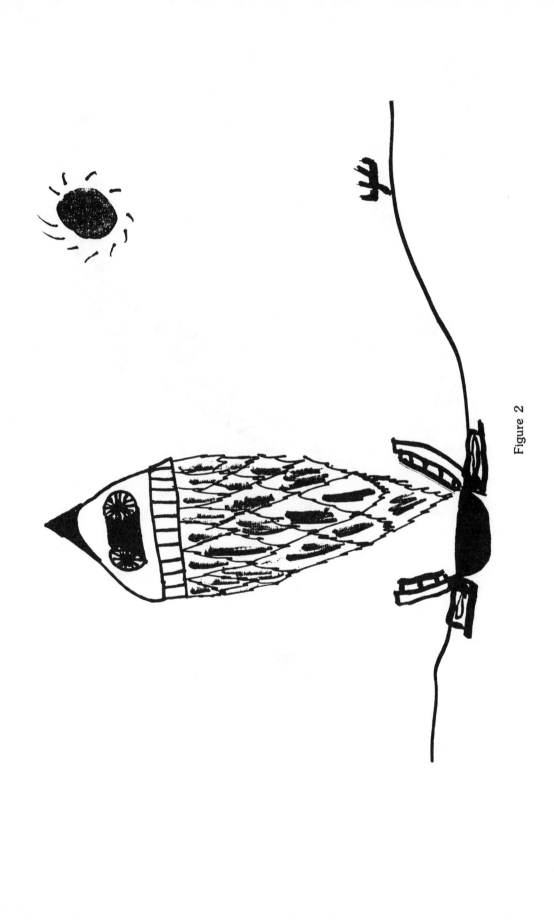

Figure 2

Figure 3

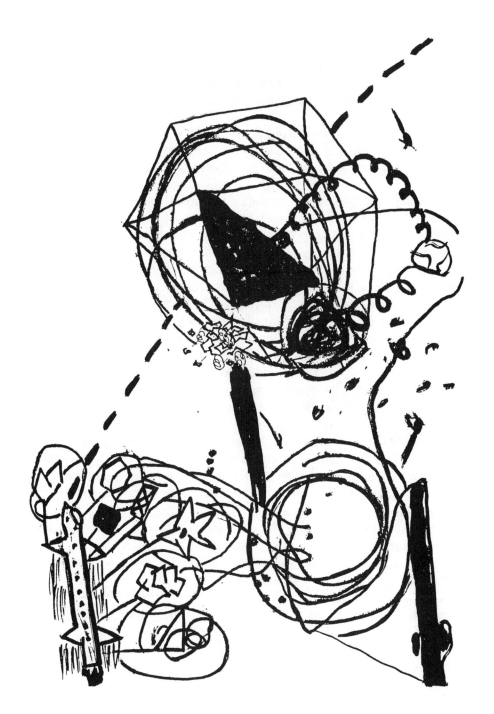

Figure 4

phorical expression as long as his defensive structure required. The artwork allowed Luke to express and share his concerns about the destructive potential in his perception of intimate closeness with another person. The consulting psychologist articulated the dynamic evident in these pictures in the following manner:

> [Luke] knows that on a deep emotional level he has a potential to be very destructive to other people and may keep a distance out of fear of destroying them or being destroyed by them.

Although Luke's space scenario obviously details his fears and fantasies, the adjunctive therapist's response must remain empathic and reflective, rather than interpretive. To interpret the material at this time would sabotage art therapy's power to guide the adolescent in his/her evolution from defensive to expressive utilization of the art materials. Undoubtedly Luke's ambivalence had its origins in his family and its metaphoric manifestation in the artwork related to the art therapist and to all the adult figures with whom he was in contact. However, rather than interpret the latent transference material, the art therapist responded to the manifest material and shared her concerns and empathy for the troubled space ship. Luke appeared to experience relief in both the intrapersonal process of symbolizing his conflicts and the interpersonal process of sharing them (however disguised).

Luke had made enormous progress in simply laying out this richly symbolic material. Because of the nonthreatening quality of the art therapy modality, he had been able to let go of his previously avoidant defenses (employed in prior psychotherapeutic contacts) and project his defensive system into a creative metaphor. This stage of art therapy treatment can be understood as a transitional bridge, utilizing defensive productions to progress from the early resistances typical of the emotionally disturbed adolescent, to more expressive productions.

Soon after completing the space battle series, Luke spontaneously switched to a different kind of artwork: less metaphorical, more directly self-representational and prompting more verbalizations. Figures 5 and 6 illustrate this new stage of art therapy treatment during which Luke was able to express his feelings of vulnerability.

Figure 5 illustrates a toothpick and Plasticine sculpture that Luke spontaneously created during one silent session. After spending over half an hour carefully constructing the fragile structure, repositioning and

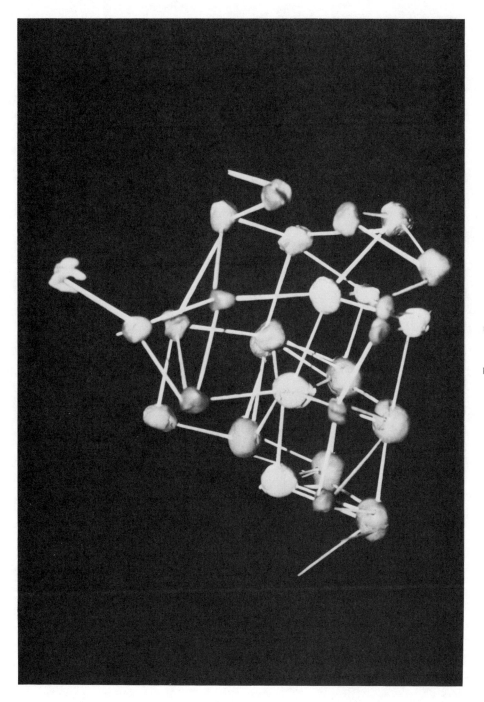

Figure 5

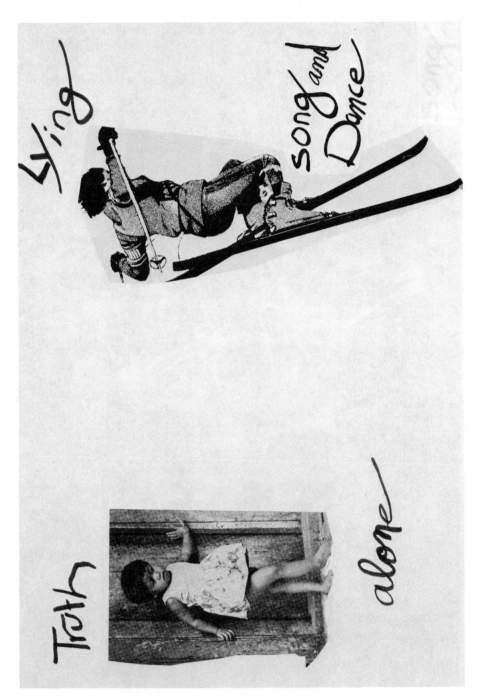

Figure 6

reconnecting each toothpick with Plasticine joints several times, Luke pointed out his inability to make it "strong enough." It was clear that the sculpture represented Luke's fragile ego structure but an interpretation at this time would have prevented Luke's next creative impulse. After sharing his frustration with the structure's weakness, Luke quickly molded a small figure out of the Plasticine and impaled it on the top toothpick of his sculpture. Jokingly he said, "This is me!" The art experience had allowed Luke to attempt genuine self-expression. Although much of the experience had been on an unconscious level, Luke had been able to recognize his own struggles in the production. It is unlikely that such an opportunity would have been available to him without the earlier metaphorical expressions of the space battle scenario. Luke had needed the opportunity, provided by adjunctive art therapy, to channel his defenses from behavioral to symbolic expression before being able to be truly expressive.

A few weeks after creating the toothpick sculpture, Luke utilized the art materials to illustrate an issue that he introduced verbally in an art therapy session. Unlike the melodramatic and distancing verbalizations of the earliest sessions, Luke's shared frustration over not being trusted in a cottage incident appeared genuine. When asked if he would like to use collage material to explore this issue, he agreed. Collage was specifically selected at this time to provide structure for Luke's first attempt to directly utilize his developing capacity to express himself artistically for self-exploration. To help him clarify the issue, the art therapist conceptualized a directive which gave form to Luke's feelings about his deceitful reputation. Luke was asked to select a picture that represented his feelings about telling the truth and then to select a picture that represented his feelings about lying. The picture on the left, a sad-looking, vulnerable waif, tells a great deal about Luke's fears of exposure, whereas the picture on the right accurately portrays the "song and dance" Luke creates to keep people distant. This collage is truly a turning point in Luke's therapy, the point in adjunctive therapy when the noninterpretive techniques have proven worthwhile. Luke has progressed from the resistant stage through the defensive stage and on to the expressive stage. At this point it is the role of the primary therapist to help Luke deal with his developing self-expression and insights. As the therapist who is also working with the family, it is up to the social worker to help the adolescent productively harness the gains of adjunctive art therapy.

It is important to point out, however, that within the model presented in this chapter, the role of the adjunctive art therapist is not over. Although Luke has made significant gains, there is a great deal of work left to do to help him let go of his defenses and further his expression. Concurrent with the working through of primary therapy, the adjunctive therapy can continue to support increasing self-expression.

Throughout Luke's participation in art therapy, the art therapist provided materials, encouragement and acceptance for self-expression. Throughout the treatment, Luke spontaneously produced artwork that not only mirrored internal struggles and experiences but also depicted an unconscious transfer of feelings which had originated in Luke's relationship to his parents. Throughout the case, the art therapist's interventions were limited either to responses to the metaphorical material (Figures 1 through 4) or to comments about the affective expression in the artwork (Figures 5 and 6). By limiting her interventions to the here and now of the art productions and the art therapy relationship, the art therapist differentiated her role from that of the primary therapist, who would attempt to connect this kind of expression to its etiology in the family.

At this point it is possible to summarize the role of the adjunctive art therapist with a modified version of the earlier cited definition of a psychotherapist in residential treatment. The new definition would read:

> [The art therapist] must set up communication, win trust, understand bizarre symbolic language and action, assess and respond to odd and perverse relationship gestures and . . . [understand the artwork as communications about] the child's early distorted and painful relationships [transferred] onto the interaction of therapist–patient. (Bettelheim et al., 1972, p. 13)

It is clear that the role of adjunctive therapist is different from that of primary psychotherapist and that of milieu therapist. Psychodynamically trained and appreciative of the unconscious projections in the artwork, but maintaining a priority on communication rather than interpretation, the adjunctive art therapist has a unique role. Problems often occur within treatment teams when this role is not fully defined or understood. This chapter has presented one model for defining the adjunctive role. Fundamental to this role is the noninterpretive manner in which responses are made to transferential material. Accepted, ap-

130

preciated and supported, transference reactions were contained within the context in which they were expressed. According to this model, it is the role of the primary therapist to help the adolescents understand the roots of these reactions, which art therapy can so successfully help them acknowledge.

6

Group Art Therapy

It has been suggested by some that group therapy is the modality of choice with the emotionally disturbed adolescent. Although this statement is responsive to the peer issues that pervade adolescent life, it oversimplifies the complexities of adolescent psychotherapy. Group therapy, as one component of a multimodality approach, does have an important role to play in the treatment of troubled youngsters. However, the selection of group therapy, either alone or in combination with other treatment approaches, must be responsive to the needs and conflicts of the particular adolescents involved. Generalized statements about the value of group therapy for all adolescents devalue the process and its power to truly benefit particular kinds of youngsters.

Group therapy with adolescent patients is often difficult and draining for therapists. Since group process is very powerful at this developmental stage, its momentum can easily become countertherapeutic and destructive. It appears that this is one of the reasons clinicians rarely find running adolescent therapy groups easy. Harnessing the adolescent's creativity and expressive potential, as is done in the art therapy modality, can direct and sustain productive group interaction.

Many authors have described the particular features of the developmental stage of adolescence that suggest why group therapy is a treatment of choice for this population. Blos (1962) most cogently delineates the issues of adolescence from a psychoanalytic viewpoint, preparing the way for other clinicians to develop therapeutic models that are responsive to the needs of this developmental stage. In his discussion of the environmental determinants of the adolescent's psychic development, he articulates the importance of the group process in the youngster's separation struggles:

> The adolescent wages a battle against authority figures with the collaborative support of the group, the influence of which mitigates superego as well as social anxiety. Through transient identification with the central person of the group, or with the egos of its members, the individual is aided in separating out the projective component from objective fact. (p. 210)

Blos's delineation of adolescent intrapsychic development supports the clinical use of group therapy in the treatment of adolescents. Several clinicians have utilized his ideas to present a psychodynamic rationale for this modality as a significant method of treatment with the teenage population. Nathan Ackerman (1955) and Irving Berkovitz (1972) offer two of the clearest formulations. Ackerman (in Esman, 1983) describes how the therapy group can offer the adolescent opportunities to develop his/her identity:

> The therapeutic group provides a social testing ground for the distorted, inappropriate perceptions of self, and relations with others, deriving from all stages of maturation. On this testing ground, the adolescent has the opportunity to put his confusion to one side and achieve some dependable, stable clarity in his personal identity. (p. 332)

Berkovitz (1972) and the authors he includes in his edited text persuasively argue for the creation of more adolescent therapy groups, seeing them as powerful tools, often in conjunction with individual and family therapy. In the prelude to the book, Irene Josselyn writes:

[The therapy group] becomes a significant arena for the adolescent in which to struggle through the confused issues that adolescence typically creates. Within this milieu it provides support against common enemies, guidelines for acceptable behavior, a forum in which to discuss issues that can be safely explored only with those who are equally unsure, and tolerance for uncertainties and inconsistencies concerning ultimate goals. (p. 3)

Art therapists have long understood the value of art expression as a catalyst for group process and a vehicle for peer communication (Landgarten, 1981; Wadeson, 1980). Since the very struggles of the adolescent revolve around self-expression and peer interaction, it seems obvious that a combination of art and group therapy techniques will be particularly effective with this population. The group modality touches the needs of the adolescent and the art modality facilitates the group process. It is a complementarity that is both curative and exciting and underlies the effectiveness of the group described in the remainder of this chapter.

The group discussed began as part of a multidisciplinary treatment team approach within a residential treatment center. It consisted of four adolescent girls who were invited to participate because of their difficulties with self-expression and peer interaction. All the girls suffered from the traumas of abusive and neglectful backgrounds and they all exhibited delinquent acting-out symptoms. Fourteen-year-old Nancy was the most aggressive and hostile of the four girls; somewhat of a ring leader, she typically encouraged peers to join her acting-out episodes, demonstrating the adolescent's utilization of the peer group for alleviation of anxiety. Thirteen-year-old Alison appeared to be more insightful and motivated than Nancy but her internal disorganization prevented her from resisting the kinds of temptations offered by Nancy and more impulsive children. Fourteen-year-old Kim was quieter and more complacent than the other group members but demonstrated a passive-aggressive relationship to authority figures. Fifteen-year-old Bonnie was the least sophisticated of the girls, and she was constantly scapegoated because of her apparent immaturity.

Each of the girls was introduced to the idea of group art therapy by the caseworker and was told that her participation was optional. It was further explained that once the girls decided to join the group, attendance would be mandatory and a commitment to continue would be expected. The group met together once a week for eighteen months, losing only one member during that time and deciding as a group to stay closed to new membership. Each week the girls produced artwork in a manner that facilitated much discussion and interaction, and adaptive methods of communication evolved over time.

To provide a framework for discussing this very complex group, Irvin Yalom's (1975) formulations regarding the theories of group psychotherapy are used. As a clear articulation of fundamental group process, these ideas help give form to the subtle and sometimes elusive dynamics witnessed in this group.

After being introduced to the idea of group art therapy by their caseworkers, each of the girls was brought to the art therapy room for an initial individual interview. Efforts were made to alleviate any anxiety the girls may have been experiencing about this new modality, in particular regarding confidentiality and inhibitions around art expression. After the process was explained and questions were answered, each of the girls was asked to produce a collage (from a box of available magazine pictures) as a means of introducing herself to the art therapist and potentially to the group. It is important to remember that although the four girls all knew each other from cottage life within the agency, the group provided them with a new interactive arena, and fresh reintroductions emphasized the sense of beginnings. Each of the girls was told that she would be asked to share her collage during the first group session.

Nancy's collage (Figure 1) illustrates this girl's typical communicative efforts prior to her participation in group art therapy. Although she had been directed to pick some pictures that told something about herself, Nancy responded to the task by requesting a black piece of background paper (only white had been provided initially) and selecting pictures from the collage box that she described as "radical." Any direct form of self-expression was very difficult for Nancy and she chose to use the art project for a defensive, somewhat oppositional retreat. The art modality not only allowed Nancy to preserve her defense, it also provided a concrete record of her self-expressive participation that could be compared to work of a later time. Nancy's collage is an example of the way the frightened adolescent can creatively utilize the art task for defensive rather than expressive communication.

136

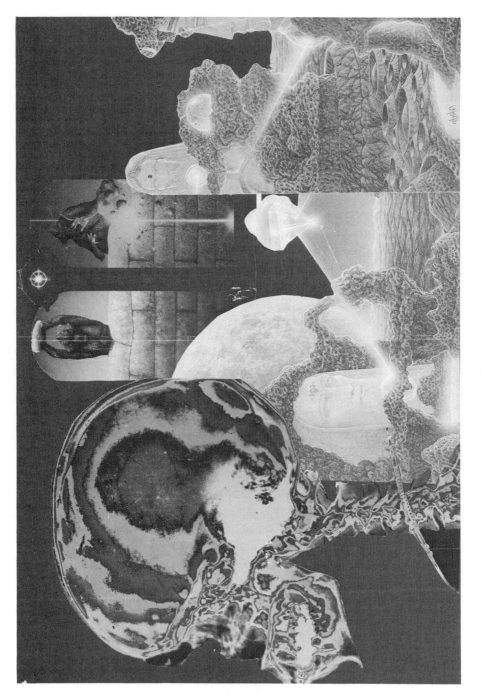

Figure 1

Alison's collage (Figure 2) also portrays a troubled youngster's difficulties with self-expression. Initially excited by the opportunity to select collage pictures about herself, Alison became panicked as she felt her suppressive hold loosen with the powerful imagery she selected. Although the images themselves suggest some of the issues at the core of Alison's difficulties (particularly her relationship with her mother's boyfriend), Alison became extremely anxious as she spoke about her collage and disassociated herself from the imagery. Alison's collage stands as a good example of how the art process can force an adolescent into a revelation of an unconscious process for which she may be unprepared. In this case, Alison was successfully able to repress the feelings evoked by the artwork. Alison would need help in modulating her progression toward increased self-expression.

Kim's collage (Figure 3) illustrates a very different response to the same directive. Intrigued by the art task and naturally very reflective, Kim spent a long time selecting her pictures and discussing the reasons for her choices. Her collage illustrates her difficulties with separation and autonomy and her struggles with development. Unlike the other girls, Kim left the initial individual interview eager to return and discuss her collage with the rest of the group members.

Bonnie had a difficult time understanding the thrust of the art directive, which had been immediately understood by the other girls. Her vague confusion was characteristic and seemed to be her defensive method of avoiding feelings and interactions by blurring their clarity. After several repeated clarifications of the task, Bonnie elected to choose pictures she liked rather than pictures that described herself. Her selection of animals (Figure 4) is typical of a younger child and illustrates this girl's characteristic manner of avoiding self-expression.

These first four collages stand as a record of each group member's early expressive abilities. Each is a unique representation of the artist's struggles with herself and each can be understood as an attempt to communicate (with varying degrees of success). The focus of the group would become efforts to help these girls unravel the distorted and discouraged communications within them. The artwork already suggested that each had a great deal to say.

The first few group sessions were structured to introduce the girls to the art materials and help them understand how the materials could be used for self-expression. The girls were encouraged to explore the

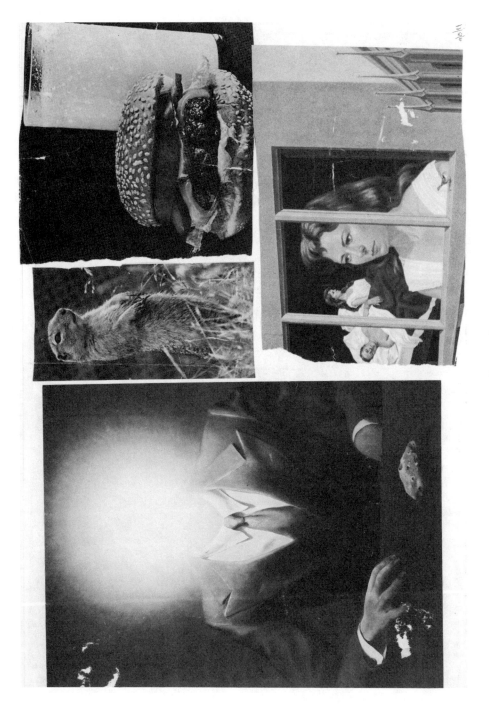

Figure 2

Figure 3

Figure 4

different media and experiment within structured kinds of exercises. It would have been very threatening to ask the girls to use the art materials directly for self-disclosure without this kind of warm-up introduction. The art projects produced during this stage of the group, stereotypical and defended, illustrated the girls' responses prior to the development of genuine group cohesion. At this early stage, intimacy remained very problematic and typical of the pseudo-intimacy of adolescents banding together in residential treatment facilities.

As each girl became increasingly comfortable in the others' presence, and less anxious about utilizing the art materials, they were asked to channel their playful expressions into directed self-expression. Art directives were conceived to help the girls explore their feelings and concerns regarding the group process. Rather than expect these youngsters to begin to use the art modality to investigate intrapsychic issues, the here and now of the group itself was the predominant focus. Yalom (1975) articulates the value of remaining within the interactions of the group when he says:

> This focus greatly facilitates the development and stark emergence of each member's social microcosm; it facilitates feedback, catharsis, meaningful self-disclosure, and acquisition of socializing techniques. (p. 122)

Directing youngsters to discuss the here and now of group process is often very difficult in verbal therapy groups. The art process allows this kind of exploration to occur: diagrams, symbols and metaphors allow the adolescent to distance herself from the potential anxiety in this kind of task.

During one of the early group sessions the four girls were asked to draw their perceptions of themselves, dividing the page into two and showing the difference between how they saw themselves as members of the group and how they saw themselves as individuals. Bonnie's drawing (Figure 5) illustrates this very troubled girl's difficulties with social interactions and her poor self-esteem. On the left she has drawn herself with a marijuana cigarette, masking her feelings of confusion and inadequacy with a symbol of acting-out peer identification. On the right she has placed herself between two peers, one verbally attacking, the other verbally defending, indicating her ambivalence about interpersonal interactions. On one page, in response to one directive, Bonnie has laid out very potent material. Since the focus of the group was not to

142

how you she yourself on one

how you see yourself in spore

I hate her

she's nice

jaint

Figure 5

interpret or even investigate the complex expressions, Bonnie's participation was first reinforced and then discussed in terms of similarities to the other girls' productions.

Nancy's drawing (Figure 6), in comparison with Bonnie's (Figure 5), offers an illustration of the way in which art tasks can facilitate group process. On the left Nancy, like Bonnie, draws herself smoking a marijuana cigarette. In fact, it was likely that Bonnie, feeling unable to come up with her own image, copied Nancy's, illustrating the ways in which Nancy provoked much of the acting-out behavior. On the right, Nancy draws herself offering marijuana cigarettes to the (unseen) other group members, suggesting through the symbols her awareness of her need to seduce her peers away from any potential genuine participation in the group. The difference between Nancy's and Bonnie's drawing offered the group an interesting take-off point for process discussion. Although the girls understood the therapist's comments regarding Bonnie's inclusion of others in her diagram of the group versus Nancy's inclusion of only herself, they were quick to deny any significance to this. Bonnie's budding ability to share affective material was squelched by Nancy's need to maintain the defenses of the group. However, despite the verbal denial and the defensive reaction, Bonnie's drawing remained concrete evidence of this early attempt at sharing feelings.

Group therapy of any sort, but particularly group therapy with adolescents, must be acutely concerned with transference issues. Because of the complicated feelings of the adolescent toward authority figures as he/she struggles with his/her own separation and individuation, transference interactions with the group leader are an important factor in the dynamics of the group. Yalom (1975) points out the inevitability of transference phenomena:

> I have never seen a group without a rich and complex underpinning of transference. The problem is, thus, not *evocation* but, on the contrary, *resolution* of transference. If the therapist is to make therapeutic use of transference, he must help the patient to recognize, to understand, and to change his distorted attitudinal set toward the leader. (p. 203) (emphases added by author)

Although Yalom's encouragement to the clinician to help the group members resolve transference issues may appear to be unrealistic with

144

in group

me alon

Figure 6

emotionally disturbed adolescents, his concepts can be utilized as a model. Irving Schulman (in Esman, 1983) helps to conceptualize the use of transference material with the adolescent population:

> In view of the lability of the disturbed adolescent's feelings, his ego limitations, his constant fear of retaliation and scorn from peers, and his easily aroused anxiety, one finds that the therapist has to take a more active role in these groups . . . If the therapist maintains reasonable control of the group situation, he will usually reduce anxieties caused by the adolescent's feelings of uncertainty and insecurity and will also encourage the development of a closer dependency relationship. (p. 387)

Adolescent transference feelings in groups are typically manifested in the form of resistances and hostility toward the therapist. The art therapy modality gives the group members an opportunity to express these feelings free to some degree from the overwhelming anxiety these feelings can generate. In addition, the art productions provide the group with a focus for exploring and reality testing their relationships with the leader.

Once the four girls had developed a familiarity with utilizing the art materials to explore issues in a directed manner, they were asked to depict their perceptions of the group leader in a drawing. This directive was not given out of context, but rather evolved from repeated expressions of hostility toward the authority figure. The potent feelings in these verbal/physical expressions were channeled and made available for exploration in the art projects.

Alison's drawing (Figure 7) of her fantasy of how she would like the therapist to interact with the group members portrays her ambivalent feelings regarding authority. She has depicted the therapist on the far left of the page, standing impotent, unable to control the marijuana smoking of the four group members. She titled the picture "Crazines" (incorrect spelling of craziness) and crossed out the title with a squiggly line. She appears caught between a wish to act out and an awareness of the "craziness" of being out of control. When this picture was compared with Kim's drawing (not shown) of a group leader in rigid control, Alison was able to acknowledge her conflictual wishes.

146

Figure 7

Nancy's drawing (Figure 8) reveals her inability to deal with authority figures and her consequent flight from real interactions toward projection, displacement and regression in the face of tremendous anxiety. This picture not only distracted her from acknowledgment of her feelings regarding the group leader, but it also provoked regression on the part of the other group members and effectively ended the group's ability to explore this issue. Once again Nancy had effectively sabotaged the group and rallied her peers into a group defense.

Hostility toward the therapist continued to be a central theme in the group sessions for some time. Very often Bonnie, however, would also become the target of the other girls' anxious displacements. Attempts to verbally explore what was going on between the group members were unsuccessful. It appeared that the unrelenting expression of negative feelings toward the therapist, as well as the scapegoating of one of the members, was an unconscious attempt to prevent the group from progressing toward genuine self-exploration. The girls were setting up a very complex obstacle and it needed to be explored before the group could move on. Consequently, an art task was utilized to help the girls express and understand the nature of the interactions.

At the core of this interaction was the youngsters' response to the too obvious vulnerability of one of their peers. Bonnie's fragile defense structure provoked anxiety among the girls and they responded with hostile projections. The art projects that resulted from this exploration illustrate how the directed art process can facilitate the resolution of these kinds of interpersonal distortions. Each girl was instructed to draw a picture of the way she saw the group interacting and the way she wanted the group to interact.

Significantly, Alison's drawing (Figure 9) of the way she observed the group interactions excluded her own self-representation from the inner circle and placed it on the outside with Bonnie and the group leader. This half of the drawing helped the group pursue a discussion about the subtleties of scapegoating and their feelings of inclusion and exclusion. The second half of Alison's drawing, where she expressed her wish that she would be in the inner circle, which would continue to exclude Bonnie and the leader, offered the group an opportunity to discuss their reasons for wanting inner and outer circles. As the girls examined these diagrammatic representations of interpersonal phenomena, they were increasingly able to discuss their feelings about the interactions.

Figure 8

THE way it is THE way I want it to be

Figure 9

Kim's drawing (Figure 10) also helped the group break out of the scapegoating pattern in which they seemed trapped. On the left side of the page Kim drew the group, showing how two of the members, Bonnie and the leader, were wiped out by the present interactions. On the right side of the paper, Kim drew a representation of her ambivalent feelings regarding Bonnie, opening the way for the group to explore the role Bonnie was playing.

Yalom (1975) discusses the very important role that group cohesiveness plays in group psychotherapy. He points out that group members' acceptance of one another may be very slow to develop but is necessary for the continuation of self-disclosure. It is even more crucial in adolescent therapy groups where peer approval is of utmost importance to the participants. In group art therapy, large group art tasks can be utilized to monitor and encourage group cohesiveness. Figure 11 is a collage done by the four members of this art therapy group to achieve that purpose.

Each girl was asked to select a picture that represented her participation in the group. We continue to see the subgrouping (Nancy, Kim and Alison apart from Bonnie) through the placement of the pictures. More importantly, we see increasing self-expression and self-disclosure as the girls respond to the group's developing cohesiveness. Despite Bonnie's continued exclusion from the inner circle, her capacity to share her vulnerability (as evidenced by her selection of a waiflike child) and the previous discussion of her feelings regarding exclusion have decreased the scapegoating. Kim, Alison and Nancy all selected pictures suggesting immersion or submergence. Kim's image appears to be moving and in control. Alison's image appears to be observing and reflecting. Nancy's image, however, appears to be in trouble, sinking further and further into the chaos. After placing her image on the collage, Nancy denied that it was a self-representation and titled it "MR. F.," defending against the anxiety engendered by this rather accurate self-portrait and displacing her feelings onto an authority figure within the agency.

Figure 11 was an important milestone for this group. It illustrated the girls' increased capacity to express themselves and it offered the girls an opportunity to confront their roles within the group.

Not surprisingly, Nancy ran away from the treatment facility after participating in group art therapy for about nine months. Although she had never lessened her defensive hold on her own self-expression and

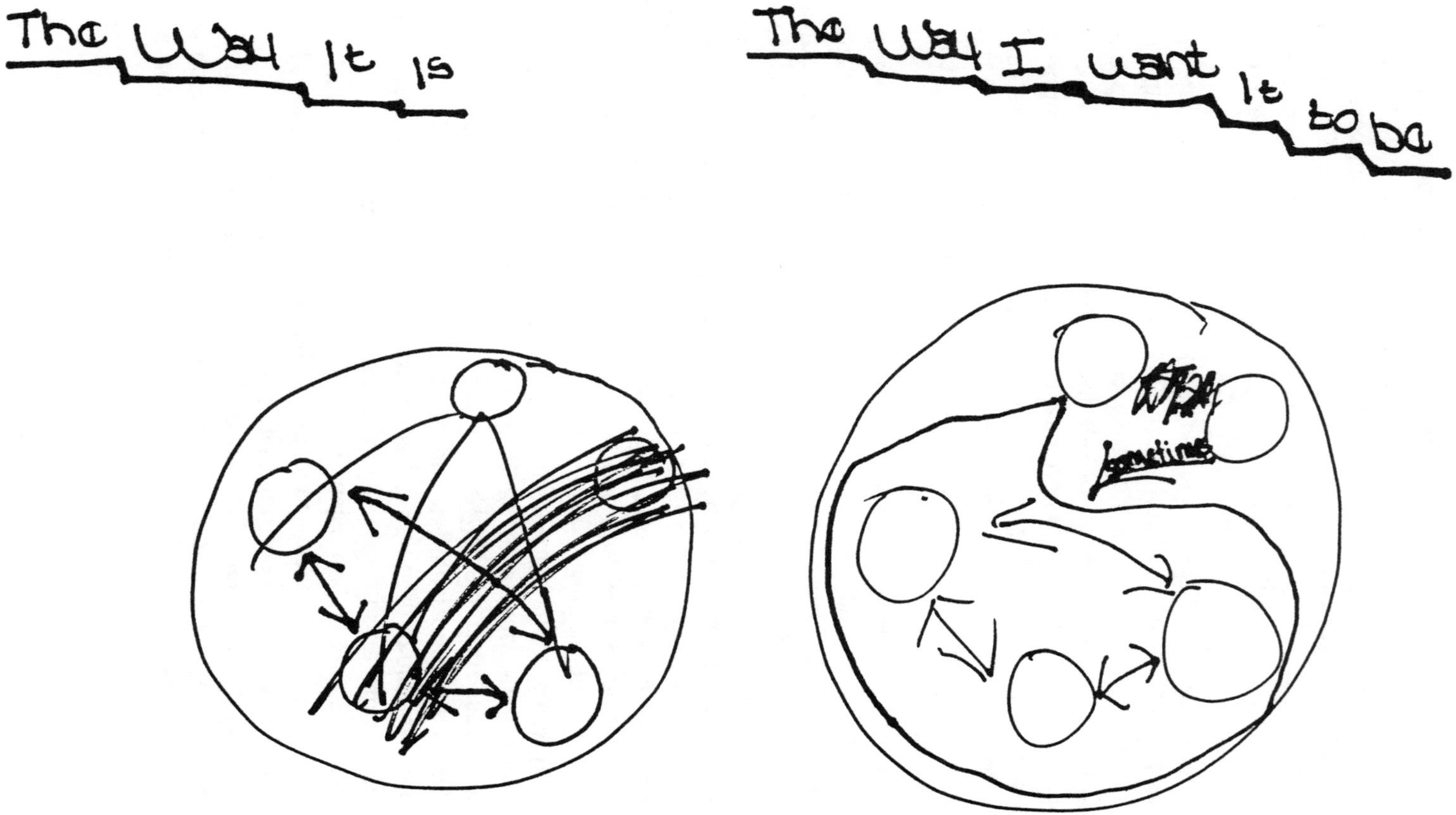

The Way It is

The Way I want It to be

Figure 10

to a lesser degree on the self-expression of the other group members, she had benefited from her participation in the group. The artwork had provided Nancy with a safe outlet for some of the intrapsychic struggles she was barely containing. Despite the fact that Nancy continued to deny any exposure, her artwork had become increasingly personal and powerful. Nancy's flight from the agency can be understood as motivated by her need to resist the self-confrontation that was being catalyzed by her increasing therapeutic investment. In essence, as her defenses weakened, her need to act out her conflicts increased, and she ran away. It is possible that group art therapy was not an appropriate modality for Nancy and her dynamics might have been more accurately assessed to prevent the provocation that likely contributed to her disappearance. However, it is also possible that Nancy in fact benefited more from her participation in group art therapy than was immediately evident and might have run away anyway.

Nancy's departure stimulated a great deal of anxiety in the other girls, feeding their own fantasies about losing control. Although most of their verbalizations expressed concern for Nancy and support for her defiance, there was little verbal access to the girls' deeper responses. The art modality provided an avenue for the girls to explore the effect that Nancy's departure had on them and on the group. In this manner, Nancy continued to play an important role in this art therapy group, despite not being physically present any longer. Yalom (1975) insists that the real value of group therapy comes from the processing of here-and-now experiences like the departure of one of the group members.

Although the girls were asked to create imagery to represent their feelings regarding Nancy's running away and their fantasies about what Nancy might be experiencing, it was significant that this directive was misunderstood and distorted in manners that were ego-syntonic for each individual.

Alison, unable to deal with the possibility that Nancy might not come back, shifted the focus of the task away from Nancy's departure and on to Nancy's return (Figure 12). Alison shared her drawing in terms of her own feelings, sad to see Nancy leave but happy to have her return. As the group discussed their drawings, it was noticed that Alison had misinterpreted the directive and the girls began discussing why Alison chose not to consider Nancy's experiences as a runaway. As the girls talked, they became increasingly aware of their own ambivalent anxiety about loss of external controls.

153

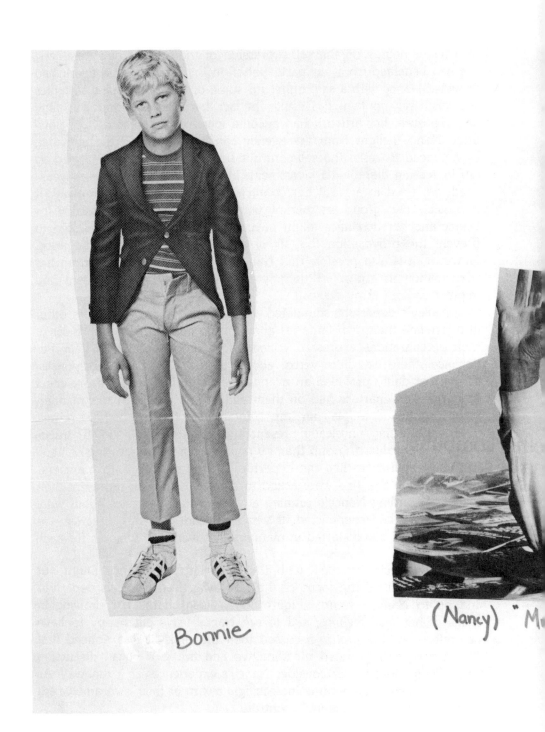

Bonnie

(Nancy) " M

Figure 11

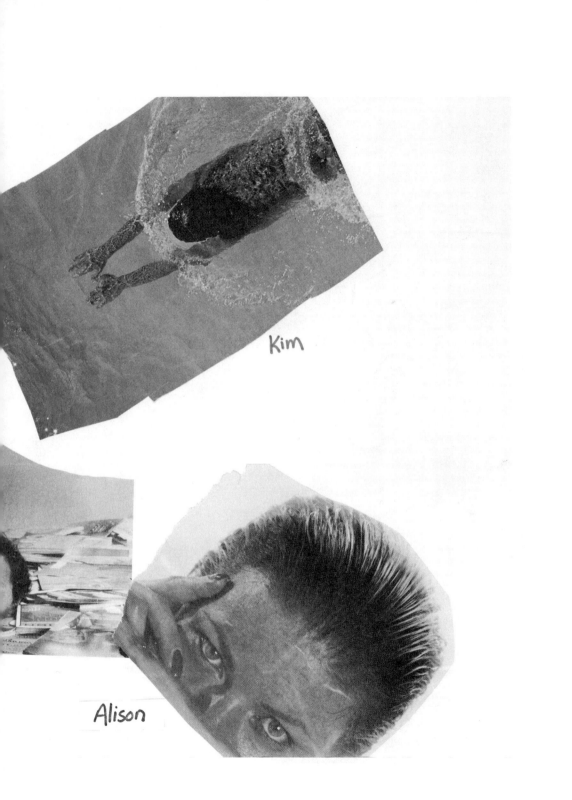

Kim

Alison

Figure 12

Bonnie's drawing (Figure 13) was also examined in the context of this discussion regarding authority. Although Bonnie depicted Nancy as "having fun" after running away, drinking beer and smoking marijuana, her own self-portrait of her mixed feelings gave the group access to Bonnie's genuine response.

As the girls' concern for Nancy's safety surfaced, so did their skepticism about her emotional health. The task of discussing Nancy's running away, facilitated by the structured art directives, led the three girls to an in-depth exploration of their own feelings about limit-setting authority figures. Once again, group process combined with art expression to encourage psychotherapeutic progress for resistive adolescents.

The group continued for almost one year after Nancy's departure from the agency. The girls decided not to increase their membership but to work instead within the framework of intimacy that had been so difficult to create. Although the group oscillated between periods of intense sharing/self-disclosure and times of very rigid resistances, it was clear that Nancy's absence did leave the group more of a working unit. Each of the three remaining girls was able to develop her unique form of self-expression and significantly expand her symbolic, communicative repertoire. Two pictures have been selected from this later stage of a working group to be compared with those earlier collages that illustrated these girls' tremendous communicative difficulties.

Bonnie's collage (Figure 14) was created in a group session when Bonnie shared her depressed feelings. Although able to verbally clarify her mood only in vague and general terms, she was able to select pictures that captured her feelings. Bonnie's selected images suggest the relationship that her current affect had with early traumas and neglect. Even without interpretation, the value of Bonnie's collage was enormous. Its very execution and her ability to share these potent images with her peers illustrate her increased capacity to tolerate her feelings and avoid the kind of interpersonal distortions her defenses had caused.

Kim's drawing of a brick wall, titled "Feeling Blocked Out" (Figure 15), was also produced once the group had clearly entered into the working stage. Yalom (1975) describes the dynamics of this stage of group therapy:

When a group achieves a degree of stability, the long working-through process begins and the major curative factors . . . operate with increasing force and effectiveness. Each member,

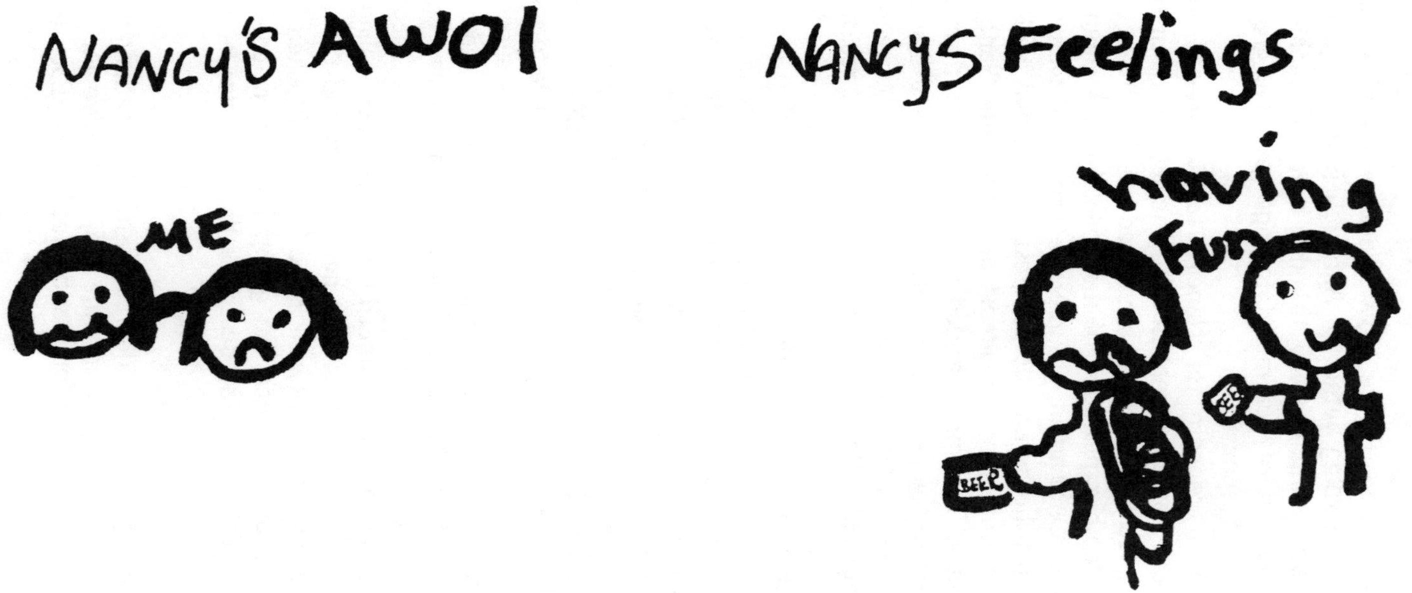

Nancy's AWOL

Nancy's Feelings

ME

having fun

Figure 13

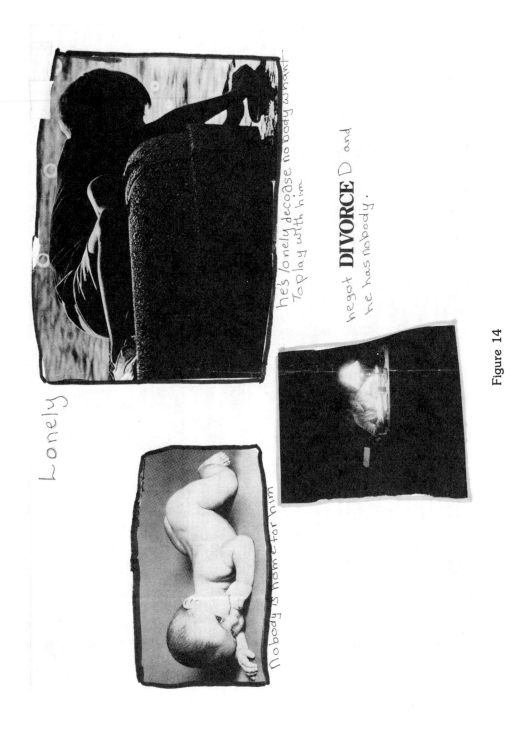

Lonely

he's lonely because nobody what
To play with him

he got **DIVORCE**D and
he has nobody.

Nobody is home for him

Figure 14

Figure 15

as he engages more deeply in the group, reveals to others
and to himself his problems in living. (p. 332)

Kim's picture (like Bonnie's collage) clearly illustrates her increased
capacity to experience self-disclosure among her peers and to explore
the subtleties of her affective life.

Group therapy cannot be fully understood without an exploration
of the termination process. Again, it is Yalom (1975) who most clearly
articulates the importance of this final psychotherapeutic process:

Termination is more than an act signifying the end of therapy
and, if properly understood and managed, may be an important
force in the instigation of change. (p. 365)

Integral to the art therapy process is the availability of the artwork
as a record of treatment during the termination process. Just as the
individual participant in art psychotherapy can review progress and
change by examining the artwork as a therapeutic calendar, so the group
members have access to concrete retrospection.

After eighteen months of participation in the art therapy group,
Kim, Alison and Bonnie were being transferred from the residential
treatment center to a group home as a transition prior to permanent
reunification with their families. Nancy had never returned to the agency
and the group of three girls had developed into a highly cohesive and
psychotherapeutic unit.

The termination process was formally introduced to the girls six
weeks before their departure from the agency. Although they obviously
had many other concurrent terminations (from caseworkers, child care
workers, administrative staff and peers) the termination from this long-
term group was important. The girls were encouraged to use the final
six-week period to review all the artwork produced in the eighteen
months and to engage in final art tasks meant to express and contain
the feelings around separation. The girls decided to progress slowly
through the artwork, each one moving from session to session at her
own pace, but on occasion directing the whole group to a particular
moment in time that interested her. The intensity of this review oscillated
from highly pitched to frivolous, suggesting that it was difficult for the
girls to sustain the introspection that the artwork potentially demanded.

Figure 16

Figure 17

Over and over again the girls exclaimed about past experiences and differences in their methods of expressing themselves. When the review reached the time of Nancy's departure, the camaraderie among Kim, Alison and Bonnie was particularly intense, as they remembered (aided by the art "souvenirs") that difficult experience.

As the girls reviewed their thick folders of art productions, there was an obvious need for external structures to contain the provoked affect. Art tasks that focused on feelings around termination were used. Figures 16 and 17 illustrate the girls' responses to this kind of directive.

Bonnie's drawing (Figure 16) depicts her perception of the changes she underwent between the beginning of the group and the end. She abstractly illustrates herself as swirling chaos in the beginning and then as chaos reintegrating at the end. Although the kind of ego development accurately diagrammed in Bonnie's simple drawing would have been impossible for her to explain verbally, her comfort with art expression, after eighteen months of participation in group art therapy, allowed her to clearly share her understanding of her progress.

Kim's collage (Figure 17) also illustrates the manner in which the artwork (both process and content) reveals psychotherapeutic progress. Kim depicts her changes as a development from the image of a distressed boy to the image of a confident-looking young woman. This imagery is particularly powerful in light of Kim's first collage, in which she portrayed her conflictual identity as child/woman. Not only does the content of her production suggest her improvement, but the process does as well. Kim executed this final collage with confidence, boldness and clarity, a far step from the hesitant little girl, so needful of help with communication.

This art therapy group had been ongoing for just over eighteen months and was a powerful experience for all involved. It stands as a clear example of how the goals of group psychotherapy with an adolescent population can be aided by utilization of the art psychotherapy modality. The art process provides an alternative mode of communication by which group cohesion can be developed, transference issues can be expressed, interpersonal learning can be facilitated, the here-and-now orientation can be processed and termination can be explored. For the adolescent patient, requiring a reality focus and a therapeutic style that does not unproductively weaken defensive structures, art expression appears to be an effective modality for group therapy.

7

Family Art Therapy

The stage of adolescence does much more than present the young-ster with a unique set of problems and developmental issues. It also affects all members of the family in which the adolescent lives. Since the essential themes of this stage of development are separation, indi-viduation and identity, the struggles that the adolescent undergoes must be understood in the context of the system which may or may not support his/her efforts. Preto and Travis (in Mirkin & Korman, 1985) point out the manner in which the intrapsychic dynamics of adolescence affect the interpersonal system of the family:

> The tasks of adolescence challenge the stability of the family system by posing new expectations and demands. Family pat-terns experience sudden and abrupt disturbances as adolescents reject and question values and defy rules while attempting to individuate. (p. 21)

165

It is the vibrant and often conflictual interplay between the adolescent and his/her family that necessitates the inclusion of the family system in the psychotherapeutic treatment of teenagers. On occasion, inclusion of the family may simply mean the therapist's thoughtful attention to the contextual framework in which his/her patient lives. On other occasions inclusion of the family may involve psychotherapeutic intervention with a portion of the family system that may not even include the adolescent identified patient. In clinical practice most treatment courses with adolescents fall somewhere between these two ends of the intra-psychic–systems continuum and involve a particular combination of individual and family treatment.

Once adolescence is understood as a process to which entire family systems are subjected and psychotherapy with adolescents is consequently understood as a balance between individual and system intervention, the potential within the family art therapy modality with this developmental stage can be clearly shown.

To illustrate the theoretical stance that underlies this chapter and demonstrate the specific techniques that are developed, case material is utilized. The case material was selected because family issues were manifest and addressed in what was begun as the individual treatment of an adolescent girl. Several art projects from a two-month period of treatment are examined in order to provide clinical illustration for the ideas in this chapter.

Jackie L. was referred for psychotherapy by her school guidance counselor. The counselor discussed the fifteen-year-old's failing grades, reckless angry attitude, and school truancy with Mrs. L. when she made the suggestion that a therapist be consulted. The suggestion resonated with Mrs. L.'s increasing frustration over her inability to communicate with and control her daughter and she agreed to seek psychotherapeutic help. Mr. L. agreed that Jackie was no longer the "good little girl" she had always been but believed that stronger disciplinary efforts on his wife's part would alleviate the problems better than intervention from a stranger. He agreed, however, to provide Jackie with psychotherapy, as long as it demonstrated "results" within three months. During most of that time, which became known within the family as the "trial period," he would be traveling throughout the country in an effort to consolidate a new business endeavor. Jackie's thirteen-year-old brother, Josh, wanted nothing to do with his sister's "problems" and felt that she should just be ignored and perhaps given more freedom. Prior to the development of Jackie's behavioral outbursts of the past year, the L. family had described themselves as "problem-free" and none of its members had a history of seeking psychiatric help. Like many families with adolescent children, Jackie's struggles for individuation and separation were reverberating throughout the system and causing havoc within a previously stable family. The following case material illustrates the manner in which the art modality provided opportunity for the therapist and for the family itself to understand and acknowledge the process it was undergoing. It also demonstrates the manner in which art tasks can be utilized to facilitate attempts to change intrafamilial functioning.

Jackie came to her first art therapy session sullen and angry. She expressed distaste for "psychology" and for "art" and claimed that the only reason she was attending the interview was that her father had promised to help get her mother "off her back" if she agreed to participate. Although Jackie refused to do any artwork for the entire first session, she did listen to the therapist's comments about families that have difficulties with teenage children and she seemed particularly attentive to the therapist's suggestion that other members of Jackie's family might be called in as needed.

Jackie returned for the second session appearing less hostile and agreed to create a collage that depicted her understanding of why she had come for therapy. On one level, her collage (Figure 1) portrays her conscious wish that the puzzle pieces of what appears to be a disjointed identity come together. On a deeper level, the puzzle metaphor and the attachment issues depicted in the puzzle pieces suggest Jackie's struggles with separation and individuation. On the left side of the collage, Jackie juxtaposes images that show a young girl developing into a young woman with the image of an infant cradled in its mother's arms positioned between the two developmental stages. Although Jackie spoke about the left side of the page in terms of her own wish to grow up and have a baby, the imagery speaks clearly about her own separation difficulties. On the right side of the page Jackie turned an image of a father playing with his two children into two pieces of her metaphorical puzzle, isolating the young girl from the other family members. Her verbal claims that she was close to her father are challenged by the manner in which she cut the collage picture, despite the fact that she emphasized the way the two parts of the puzzle "fit so nicely together." In the lower right portion of the collage a picture of a dove entitled "Freedom" reflects Jackie's concerns with her own autonomy. Asked to create a title for

Figure 1

her piece, Jackie selected the words "No Pain, No Gain," indicating her own understanding of the conflictual process she was undergoing. The collage as a whole is a powerful expression of an adolescent's struggles between family ties and autonomous development and was the first in a series of individual artwork that provided the therapist with concrete tools to help Jackie and her family support rather than symptomatize her conflicts.

Jackie was seen in individual art therapy for several sessions, establishing a relationship with the therapist and becoming increasingly comfortable with the modality. As the issues of separation and individuation became clearer and easier for her to acknowledge, it became apparent that her family's support was required for conflict resolution. Jackie's drawings also suggested that her family members were caught in conflictual responses to her adolescent efforts. Family therapy would likely stir up a great deal of feelings and needed to be approached thoughtfully. Frank Williams (in Esman, 1983) articulates the underlying issues that can resonate in a family system when an adolescent child begins to individuate:

> The adolescent, in his struggle to achieve freedom from his family, often threatens, within himself and his parents, very primitive fears of object loss and separation from symbiotic involvements. (p. 283)

Although scheduling family therapy was a tremendously difficult task, involving confrontation of Mr. L.'s travel agenda and other manifestations of the family's resistance, a conjoint session was able to be arranged. In the only interview in which the therapist was able to meet with all four members of the L. family, the art therapy modality proved to be a powerful tool in defusing the identified patient role assigned to Jackie by her family. Figures 2, 3 and 4 were created by Jackie's brother, father and mother, respectively, in response to the therapist's encouragement for each of them to depict his or her understanding of the family's current functioning. In all of these collages the confusion generated by Jackie's struggle between dependence and independence is evident.

In Figure 2, thirteen-year-old Josh depicted the ambivalent expression of the L. family's younger generation. Although the words of the child he selected as a self-representation are captioned as "Why dou [sic] treat me like a baby?," the image itself is infantile. An apparent

Figure 2

spokesperson for the family's conflicts with separation, Josh seemed to be speaking for both himself and his sister. His collage was examined by the whole family for its double message, thereby providing the system with concrete metaphor for the family struggles. Although Josh refused to return for any more sessions, he had played a very valuable role as issue focuser.

Mr. L.'s collage (Figure 3) depicts this troubled father's reaction to his daughter's strivings for identity and independence. The avoidance maneuvers he adopted in relationship to his family, fortified by his business endeavors, hint at his intrapsychic stress. Williams (in Esman, 1983) articulates the manner in which parents often experience the struggles of their adolescent children:

> The sexual conflicts stirred up within the adolescent by nature of his physical and psychosexual growth often lead to the development of dramatic distancing mechanisms between parents and their sons and daughters. (p. 284)

In his collage Mr. L. placed self-representational images on either side of the page, explaining the man on the right as "checking in on the home situation from afar" and the man on the left as "pinned to the wall immediately after returning home." Interestingly, he positioned the picture of the nurturing family of horses between these two images. Attachment imagery is at the center of this collage, just as attachment imagery was at the center of Jackie's collage, and just as attachment is the central issue for this distressed family. Unfortunately, Mr. L.'s maladaptive coping mechanisms, avoidance and distancing seem to have caused further family stresses, particularly within the parental relationship. Mr. L.'s collage hints at the marital tensions that have been exacerbated by Jackie's adolescence. Similar to the imagery of his daughter, Mr. L.'s artwork suggests his ambivalence toward separation, as well as the family's as a whole. Once again the artwork served as an aid in family assessment and as a facilitator for the acknowledgment and consequent discussion of important issues.

An equally powerful statement about the family's difficulties with separation is Mrs. L.'s collage (Figure 4) produced in the same session. Although Mrs. L. explained her production as a statement about the manner in which she tries to keep things running smoothly in the family, the imagery suggests marital tension and skewed family alliances. Sig-

171

Figure 3

Figure 4

nificantly Josh is not included in this picture, because, according to Mrs. L., he is uninvolved in the family's current difficulties. Jackie is depicted as a clinging young child, a repeated and important misrepresentation throughout the L. family's imagery. Both Jackie and Mrs. L. are depicted calling out to Mr. L., who, despite his wife's and daughter's attempts, appears to be abandoning the situation. Mrs. L. became tearful as she discussed this collage and increasingly acknowledged its suggestions of marital conflict. Although Jackie was initially angry toward her mother for representing her as such a young child, her affect changed as she witnessed her mother's sad recognition of her own feelings of abandonment.

The remainder of the session was spent discussing the three collages created by Jackie's family members. Josh's ambivalence (Figure 2), Mr. L.'s isolation and sense of exclusion (Figure 3) and Mrs. L.'s anger (Figure 4) became the focus of the discussion which attempted to reformulate Jackie's symptoms in a family systems framework. It appeared that Mr. L.'s distress over his daughter's psychosexual growth had caused him to withdraw from the family. This withdrawal exacerbated the dissatisfaction Mrs. L. was experiencing within the marriage and much of her anger became displaced onto Jackie, simultaneously the cause and the victim of the family discord.

As a result of the powerful and revealing session in which Figures 2, 3 and 4 were produced, specific treatment goals were formulated. Mr. and Mrs. L. were encouraged to seek marital counseling in an effort to separate the complexities of their relationship from the family's response to Jackie's adolescent struggles. In addition, future sessions with Jackie and each of her parents alone were scheduled in an attempt to help both adults support Jackie's efforts at separation and individuation. The power of such an intervention is implied in Frank Williams's (in Esman, 1983) cautionary remarks about the adolescent's potential resistance to parental support:

> The family can often be helped to encourage the teenager toward independent individuation; the teenager's role in undermining that potential encouragement from his parents is most observable for confrontation in family meetings. (p. 288)

Figure 5 is a dual drawing created jointly by Jackie and Mrs. L. in the next session, which only they attended. At the beginning of the

174

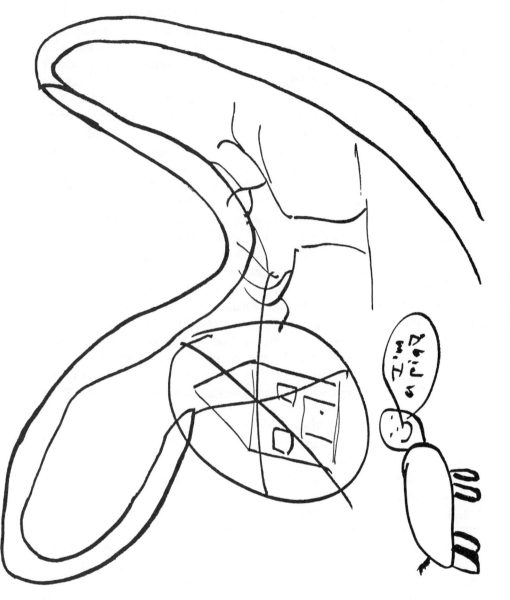

Figure 5

session they were instructed to create a drawing together, each using a different color and not talking until the drawing was completed. Figure 5 was executed rapidly; Jackie waited silently while mother used a black marker to draw a house, a tree and a path, subsequently pausing in anticipation for Jackie's additions. Horrified by her daughter's use of a red marker to immediately cross out the house and represent her mother as a pig, Mrs. L. exclaimed that the drawing was over and that its execution had been exactly like everything that went on between mother and daughter at home. An examination of the drawing, however, revealed a maladaptive pattern in the mother–daughter interactions: Mrs. L.'s latent restrictive expressions hidden within her manifest encouraging communications. Although she was ostensibly attempting to create a "pretty scene" that "could include her daughter," it became obvious that Jackie had little opportunity to do anything but follow (or be contained by) her mother's path. Reacting unconsciously to the entrapment depicted in mother's drawing, Jackie became angry and provocative. Consequently Mrs. L. and Jackie were encouraged instead to work on separate pieces of paper, creating messages that they wanted to give to each other. Their completed drawings (not shown here) were successful expressions of concern and caring, executed in very different styles and with very different imagery. Once again, the artwork created in the session provided the focus for the discussion between the L. family members. In this session, Mrs. L. and Jackie discussed the manner in which daughter experienced mother's expectations. It was hoped that as Mrs. L. benefited increasingly from marital counseling, she would be able to understand how her own dependency needs had a constraining effect on Jackie's growing independence. At the present time, she was encouraged to simply recognize the way mother and daughter had separate styles, separate messages and separate goals.

The following session was attended by Jackie and Mr. L. and once again the two participants were asked to create a nonverbal dual drawing (Figure 6). It is interesting that Jackie selected a color (light blue) very close to the one chosen by her father (dark blue) but had earlier selected a color (red) that directly contrasted with her mother's choice (black). In this session's drawing, Mr. L. began structuring the boxes on the left side of the page, apparently ignoring his daughter, and Jackie began a similarly geometric construction formed from the words "Rock" (for rock music). Mr. L. paid very little attention to his daughter's clear attempts to connect, at least stylistically, within the drawing and in fact

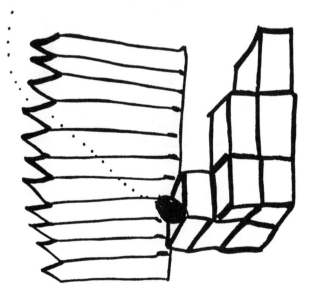

Figure 6

Figure 7

further isolated himself from Jackie by outlining a fence behind his construction. As her father drew his fence, Jackie picked up the red marker (the color she had used previously when drawing angrily with her mother) and colored in the letters of her "Rock" construction. When her father did not respond to this blatant rule breaking (task had clearly stipulated that each retain only one color for the entire drawing), Jackie drew a tentative line from her construction over her father's fence and ended with a "dropped bomb" on her father's geometric design. In this carefully observed drawing process it was obvious that Jackie's initial identification/communicative efforts were ignored, likely because of their adolescent tone. Her second attempt to engage her father (rule breaking) was also unsuccessful and she tried a third time, using the imagery for direct provocation.

The discussion that followed this drawing process focused on the manner in which Jackie attempted to stay connected with her father as she struggled with her own yearnings for separation. As the discussion continued Mr. L. was increasingly able to share his feelings of sadness over the loss of his "little girl." The explorations of this session were of enormous help in Jackie's understanding of her parents' emotional responses to the complex adolescent stage she was experiencing. In addition, the discussion helped Mr. L. understand both his own defensive maneuvers of withdrawal and the manner in which his retreat affected his daughter's separation struggles.

In the previous three sessions, various combinations of the L. family produced artwork together in an effort to provide the family with concrete tools to help them acknowledge the manner in which Jackie's difficulties were interrelated with family issues. It had become clear that to help Jackie, the identified adolescent patient, the therapist needed to help the entire family struggle with the issues of adolescence. The collage tasks and the consequent discussions proved an excellent technique for this important goal of therapy with adolescents.

In her first individual art therapy session subsequent to the family meetings, Jackie created the collage shown in Figure 7 in response to the therapist's request to depict her understanding of what she had learned from the family meetings. This collage reflects the increased empathy Jackie had gained for her parents over the difficult process of family art therapy. Although the central image of this collage is a question mark, suggesting Jackie's concerns about the future, she included images that poignantly reflect increased acknowledgment of family issues. The

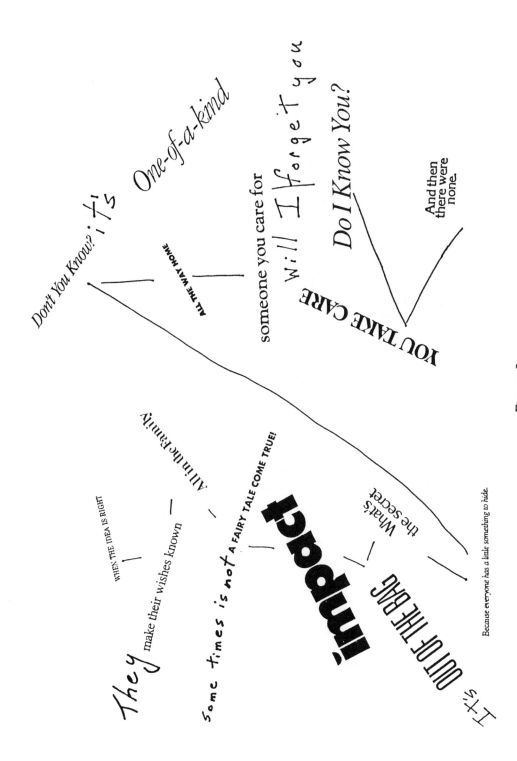

Figure 8

image on the left side of the collage, selected to represent mother's feelings of impotence, and the image on the right side of the collage, selected to represent father's sense of exclusion, are both testament to Jackie's increased insight into the family situation. In addition, the collage as a whole appears more integrated and more richly expressive than her first production (Figure 1).

Jackie remained in treatment for several more months, continuing to work on issues of identity and separation. Both her parents were periodically invited to attend sessions as Jackie felt the need to share newly recognized feelings in the supportive atmosphere that psychotherapy had become for her. As she progressively established herself as an emotionally separate entity from her parents, her need to provoke and antagonize them decreased. Although Mr. and Mrs. L. benefited only minimally from the marital counseling which they predictably terminated prematurely, the referral itself had played the important function of delineating intragenerational from intergenerational conflicts.

Treatment had taken longer than the three-month "trial period" originally contracted by Mr. L., but significant changes had occurred. Although Jackie continued to be riddled with ambivalence about her sexuality and concerns for her future, she had begun to discover herself through her self-expressive productions. Deciding on her own to terminate art therapy, she created a "goodbye" collage (Figure 8) to depict the changes she perceived herself to have undergone. On the left side of the page, Jackie created a powerful expression of the manner in which the sharing and uncovering of denied family affect had relieved her. On the right side of the page, Jackie continued her technique of word collage to express her closeness to the therapist, her ally in the self-discovery process art therapy had provided for her.

The art therapy treatment of Jackie L. illustrates the manner in which a balance between individual and family therapy must be established in response to the unique needs of each adolescent patient. Just as it is an error to ignore the familial context of an adolescent's separation struggles, it is also an error to ignore the adolescent's profound needs for an empathic one-to-one ally. The adolescent therapist must include the family when conceptualizing treatment and must adopt a flexible framework that can harness that conceptualization of the "adolescent family" in a practical manner.

8

Clinical Study

This clinical study investigates the art therapy productions of ten severely emotionally disturbed adolescents who are participating in a comprehensive mental health day treatment program. Over a five-month period the relationship between the adolescents' self-expressive attempts (as evidenced in their art productions) and their observable behavior (as evidenced in the milieu) is examined. This study provides an understanding of the manner in which self-expressive abilities affect and are affected by participation in intensive treatment programs. To provide clinical support for the development of this understanding, the changes in self-expressive abilities demonstrated in the art productions of these ten youngsters are compared with changes observed in the other components of their treatment.

This clinical study was conducted at the Dubnoff Center for Child Development and Educational Therapy, North Hollywood, California.

The limitations of this project, its small size and the absence of systematic procedure, severely restrict its theoretical importance. It is an exploratory study, designed to investigate the role that the art productions can play in helping the treatment team understand the often perplexing patterns of adolescents within intensive milieu treatment programs.

Treatment occurred within the day treatment/day school component of a residential treatment program designed to serve severely disturbed adolescents in need of out-of-home placements or at risk of institutional placement. In addition to a structured residential program, the adolescents were provided with specialized intervention within an integrated day treatment educational and therapeutic program. The goals of this integrated approach were threefold: to facilitate movement toward the highest possible level of functioning, to prevent rehospitalization or reinstitutionalization, and to discourage dependency and chronicity. The day treatment component of this program was staffed by a multidisciplinary team that included an administrator, a psychologist, a social worker, a psychiatrist, a nurse, a teacher, a teacher's aide, a behavioral specialist, an art therapist and several support staff of the larger special education day school of which this program was a part. All the youngsters in the program came into contact with all the staff members giving them the opportunity to develop supportive and psychotherapeutic relationships throughout the milieu. Staff reported regularly to each other about each adolescent's progress in order to sustain the treatment team approach.

PROCEDURE

This clinical study was begun in September 1986 with the ten youngsters currently participating in the program. For five months efforts were made to collect data that could facilitate a comparison of the adolescents' self-expressive development with their behavior in the milieu. To do this, recording procedures were developed for the treatment team members and, over the same time period, the art therapy productions of each of the adolescents were saved.

At the beginning of the clinical study each of the participants was given the same open-ended art directive in an effort to assess his/her self-expressive capacities previous to art therapy intervention. This initial task directed the youngster to select cut-out magazine pictures from a basket provided and create a collage that described him/herself. The directive was given in the initial art therapy session and provided a basis for comparison of observable progress in self-expression as evidenced in subsequent sessions.

All the treatment team members were provided with forms to record their observations of the children's behavior and emotional functioning. Team members were encouraged to update these forms each month (for five months) as the art therapist collected the adolescents' art productions over the same time period. At the end of five months the youngsters were requested to repeat the original art directive to assess changes in self-expressive abilities.

Although the assessment of the adolescents' artwork was subjective (i.e., therapist and researcher were the same individual) and the observations of the treatment team were not systematically collected, the relationship between these two components was noteworthy and provided an interesting basis for analyzing each participant's treatment process. As the clinical study proceeded, it became increasingly clear that the art productions related to the behavioral observations made by the treatment team members who daily interacted with the children. The case material which follows examines the varied manifestations this relationship can take and illustrates the manner in which self-expressive abilities correspond with participation in intensive milieu treatment.

All ten children in this project were referred from the Los Angeles County Department of Mental Health and Department of Children's Services and all were dependents of the Court. Backgrounds include severe neglect, physical and sexual abuse and multiple abandonments. In addition to the emotional handicaps of the participating adolescents, each had experienced educational difficulties and had been labeled as mildly or moderately mentally retarded by previous clinicians. Overall the youngsters' deprivations, cognitive impairments and traumatic histories combined to present a clinical picture of highly defended adolescents with limited capacity for insight.

For some of the youngsters art psychotherapy became a nonthreatening vehicle for psychotherapeutic exploration, whereas for others it primarily offered an opportunity for contained relationship. However, for all the adolescents involved in the program, the art therapy modality provided an opportunity to assess change (or lack of change) in self-expressive abilities. The remainder of this study presents case material on each of the ten participants to illustrate the manner in which the art

185

productions correlate with the observations of the treatment team. Discussion emphasizes the way the artwork depicts both the external controls and the internal conflicts of the adolescents. The relationship between changes in self-expressive abilities as manifest in art psychotherapy and changes in behavior as manifest in milieu participation is examined.

The art productions examined were all created in individual art therapy sessions in which the adolescents were encouraged to freely select art materials (from a range of simple two- and three-dimensional media) and utilize them in any manner they wished. The artwork does not stand independent of the therapeutic relationship which facilitated the creative process. Productions were encouraged, discussed and sometimes even directed by the therapist as each adolescent evidenced increased ability to develop self-expression.

The behavioral observations were recorded on forms intended to organize team members' assessment of each adolescent's evolving capacity for relationship, behavioral controls and direct expression of feelings.

THE CASE MATERIAL

Sam

Sam is a sixteen-year-old boy with a history of educational failures and repeated diagnoses of a variety of psychotic disorders. Currently unwanted by mother and the new family she recently created with stepfather, Sam feels emotionally supplanted and reports ongoing physical abuse in the home.

In the initial art task, Sam created a collage (Figure 1) that suggests very limited ability at self-exploration. The imagery he selected to represent himself symbolically depicts his concerns with controlling his explosive outbursts of aggressive conflicts. The picture in the center appears to portray Sam's introjection of the institutional process as a way of helping him regulate the expression of affect hinted at in the fiery bottom image. The top picture seems to represent the explosive outbursts that Sam has difficulty containing. Although this collage is a powerful expression of the adolescent's intrapsychic process, suggesting the boy's potential to utilize metaphorical self-expression, Sam was unable to acknowledge any connection to his own experiences.

186

Figure 1

The treatment team initially found Sam to be relatively easy to manage in the classroom but unavailable for interactions that involved intimacy and self-expression. Over five months very little change in this original description was observed. Sam's participation in art therapy also reflected minimal progress but did seem to offer a controlled outlet for the boy's internal conflicts. Just as the treatment staff was observing a compliant but apparently detached (internalizing) youngster, his involvement in the art process suggested his preoccupations with intrapsychic material.

For the first few months of art therapy Sam elected to use Plasticine, molding and remolding aggressive monsters that engulfed one another in violent dramas. Never allowing any of his creatures to be saved, recreated or developed, Sam appeared to be utilizing this "play" as an outlet for his aggressive/destructive feelings. Eventually Sam took increasing interest in the drawing materials and began to create imagery that reflected a more settled capacity for permanent (i.e., not immediately destroyed) self-expression.

Figures 2 and 3 are characteristic of Sam's evolving use of the art modality for projective imagery. Begun as spontaneous scribbles, they were completed with the therapist's encouragement to develop the imagery and the story. Sam wrote on the back of Figure 2, "The skeleton is asking a genie for a family." On the back of Figure 3 he wrote, "The genie said, 'That is too much to ask for. No more wishes.'" These sketchy drawings suggest Sam's abandoned, hopeless and confused feelings, although the affect remained unacknowledged. Simultaneous with Sam's increased capacity to metaphorically disclose his turbulent feelings, a very slight increase in acting-out behavior was observed by the classroom staff. It is possible that his anxiety over an unconscious recognition of intrapsychic disclosures in the art productions catalyzed his less containable behavior.

Sam's final collage (Figure 4) reflects little improvement in his self-expressive capacity. His selected imagery remains as bizarre and disconnected from his apparent experiences as the pictures in his first collage. It appears that the therapeutic opportunity provided for Sam in his art therapy experience involved the undirected art process in which the youngster could take advantage of primary process art activities to release turbulent material. Just as little change was observed in his behavior within the milieu, little progress in his self-expressive abilities was evidenced in his art productions.

The skeleton is asking
a genie for a family

Figure 2

The genie said,
"That is too much to
ask for. No more
wishes."

Figure 3

Figure 4

Johnny

Johnny is a fourteen-year-old boy, the oldest of four children born to a mentally retarded mother determined by the court to be an unfit parent. After being removed from the home because of filth, neglect and allegations of sexual abuse, placement had been difficult for Johnny and he had attempted suicide on numerous occasions in previous facilities. Although described repeatedly in his records as mentally retarded, it became apparent that his cognitive dysfunction related primarily to his emotional deprivations.

In the initial art task (Figure 5), Johnny clearly depicted his impulsivity. Unable to contain his production within the boundaries offered, Johnny required additional paper to include all the imagery he selected. His collage portrays the unfocused and distractible manner in which this impulsive adolescent operates. Predominantly aggressive images combine with the hospital picture on the lower left to present an expression of how this youngster allows his impulsive behavior to defend against acknowledgment of his inner vulnerability. Like Sam's collage, Johnny's imagery portrays the potential art therapy offers for adolescents unable to directly express intrapsychic concerns.

The treatment team initially found Johnny to be an impulsive, difficult boy who nonetheless was able to evoke strong attachments and concern on the part of all the staff members. Over five months significant changes were observed by the treatment team as Johnny's behavior worsened, his anxiety escalated and, somewhat paradoxically, his relationships with staff deepened. His artwork delineates and perhaps makes sense of this troubling pattern.

Figure 6 depicts the chaotic internal state that was underlying Johnny's acting-out behaviors. The imagery is full of anxiety, destruction, rage and lack of containment and accurately reflects the boy's undeveloped, disorganized ego. As Johnny subsequently pulled away from spontaneous art projects that too clearly mirrored his disturbances, he found opportunity to utilize this modality in more structured projects. It is interesting to note that the milieu staff observed parallel increases in his attachment capacity as he increasingly took advantage of art materials that allowed him to retain control. Over the five months of this clinical study, Johnny developed from tactile play involving object permanency (gluing over lumps of Plasticine), through competitive games involving mastery and control (interactive drawings with the therapist), through

192

initial efforts at self-representation (paper folding following specific instructions in an origami book). This evolving process appears to delineate Johnny's developing comfort and growth within an intimate relationship. However, as he responded to the nurturing and caring efforts of the milieu staff, Johnny apparently reacted somewhat differently. Unable to find ways (as he had in the art projects) to control his experiences, Johnny became overwhelmed by his increasing intimacy and consequent self-disclosure. As a result his anxiety escalated and he became increasingly, rather than decreasingly (as might have been expected) out of control. It is likely that Johnny was unequipped to handle the demands of psychotherapeutic progress.

Johnny's final collage (Figure 7) illustrates the progress which was witnessed only paradoxically by the treatment team members. The randomly explosive imagery has disappeared and with his picture selections Johnny was able to clearly and directly express his sadness, his anger, his pain and his ongoing concerns about medication. His ability to express himself and to verbally acknowledge his experiences, as evidenced in this collage, suggest tremendous progress from his earlier limited participation. In addition, this self-expressive improvement explains Johnny's increased anxiety (manifested behaviorally) as he unsuccessfully attempts to process increased self-awareness. With this adolescent, the art productions can augment the treatment team's understanding of the behavioral changes they observed.

Brian

Brian is a sixteen-year-old boy who experienced a long series of placements consequent to his extrusion from the family of origin at the time of his parents' separation. Allegations of early physical abuse contribute to this adolescent's defensive posture and limited cognitive functioning.

In the initial art task (Figure 8), Brian's selection of a picture of a dog absorbed in a television screen coupled with representations of money suggest his difficulties with self-expression. The collage represents the maneuvers that this adolescent uses to distract and avoid intimacy and consequent self-disclosure.

The treatment team initially found Brian to be very responsive to the milieu structure and available for relationships of limited intimacy. Over five months the team members noticed little change except for a

193

Figure 5

194

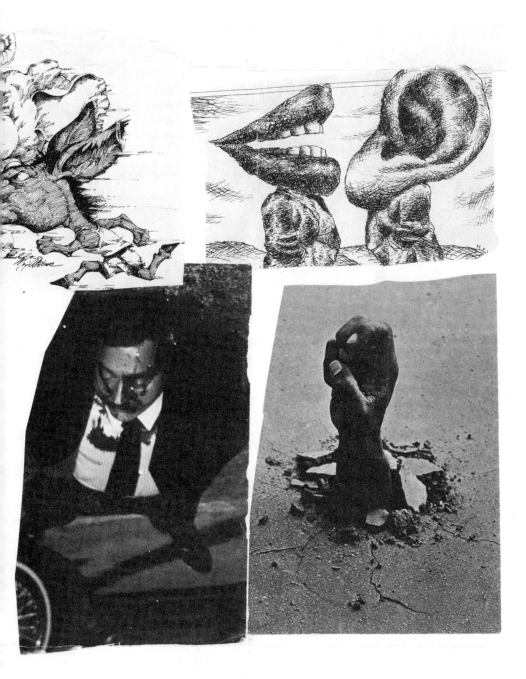

Figure 6

196

197

Figure 7

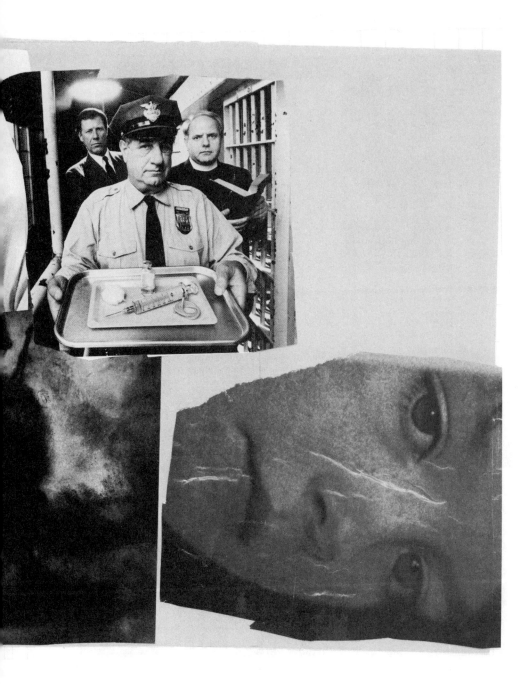

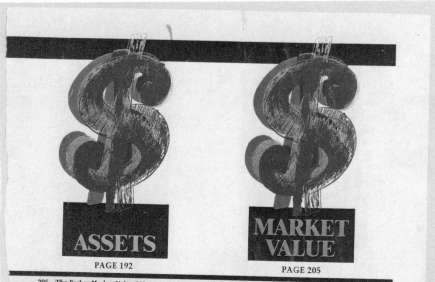

ASSETS
PAGE 192

MARKET VALUE
PAGE 205

Figure 8

slight improvement in behavioral controls and in relationships with staff. It appears that Brian felt comfortable within the structure/containment of the treatment milieu. An understanding of how this youngster utilized the milieu to bolster his self-control helps demystify his increasing intolerance for participation in the art therapy modality.

After two months of defended involvement in the art process, Brian began a project that was to evoke uncontrolled self-expression and a consequent retreat from this psychotherapeutic approach. Figures 9 and 10 present two pages from a book he created about his personal history, a project suggested by the therapist in an inaccurate assessment of his limited ability to tolerate resurfaced affect. The power of these images deeply affected Brian, and his declining willingness to participate in art therapy began with the expression of anger toward the art therapist. Increasingly hostile, Brian eventually refused to speak with the therapist and, in a very primitive use of the defense mechanism of splitting, appeared to identify her as the representation of all the unacceptable feelings against which he was so tenaciously defending. Despite, or perhaps because of, his rejection of the self-expressive potential in art therapy, Brian was able to integrate the structure of the treatment approach in an apparent fortification of his defense mechanisms. The complex task of improving external controls while recognizing internal conflicts was apparently too difficult for Brian. In this example, the resistance to the self-expressive potential in art psychotherapy paralleled the boy's increasingly defensive (and increasingly successful) participation within the milieu.

Jim

Jim is a fifteen-year-old mentally retarded boy with a severe emotional disturbance. Raised by an equally limited mother and an alcoholic father, Jim appears to have experienced early but undocumented sexual abuse and presents as confused, disorganized and absorbed with internal stimuli.

In the initial art task (Figure 11), Jim illustrated his disorientation and difficulties with reality testing. The images he selected had no relationship to his descriptions of them and his disconnected associations suggested his preoccupation with internal rather than external experiences.

201

Figure 9

Figure 10

Figure 11

The treatment team initially found Jim to be extremely limited and unavailable for relationship. However, over five months the team members observed an overall improvement in his interactions with both staff and peers despite little change in his ability to express his feelings. Participation in art therapy became a unique experience for this boy, who seemed more obviously responsive to the reality oriented, nurturing efforts of the milieu staff.

The collages in Figures 12 and 13 are characteristic of Jim's participation in art therapy. Continuing to rely on collage pictures to initiate his self-expressive attempts, this very limited youngster seized randomly selected imagery as a vehicle for the projection of repetitive material. Apparently less responsive to the collage pictures than to internal imagery that seemed to be a constant part of his reality, Jim used his art therapy experience in a unique manner. In essence, this modality became a safety-valve opportunity for the ventilation of extremely difficult and obsessive material, the violent and sexual victimization of vulnerable children. It is possible that this self-expressive outlet allowed Jim to free himself of some of his internal preoccupation and consequently provide himself with the emotional energy for the slight improvement observed by the treatment team. With this adolescent, the increasing potency of his self-expression can be correlated with his increasingly controlled behavior as he was able to take advantage of the potential within art therapy to relieve himself of overwhelming conflicts.

Ernest

Ernest is a seventeen-year-old boy diagnosed at intake by the consulting psychiatrist with residual schizophrenia and mild mental retardation. Raised by transient carnival workers, it appears that Ernest was severely abused by a mentally ill father.

In the initial art task (Figure 14), Ernest's selection of a singular image and his subsequent rejection of its self-representational meaning (crossing out and attempting to undo his selection) suggest his unmet dependency needs and the defenses he employs to guard against the experiencing of those needs. His collage is a poignant representation of an adolescent emerging into adulthood but still struggling with residual infantile issues. The powerful but unacknowledged material in this collage suggests Ernest's potential availability for self-understanding through his art productions.

205

He's in the County Jail.
because he raped his
wife. He's going to stay
in jail for 20 years
until he tells the truth.

Figure 12

The mom played with matches
She burned the house. She killed
her kids. She tied both hands up, put
gags over their mouth, put gasoline around
the driveway, took them to a junkyard and put
the car in a crusher. She'll pay for that when
the police catch her.— for 20 years.

Figure 13

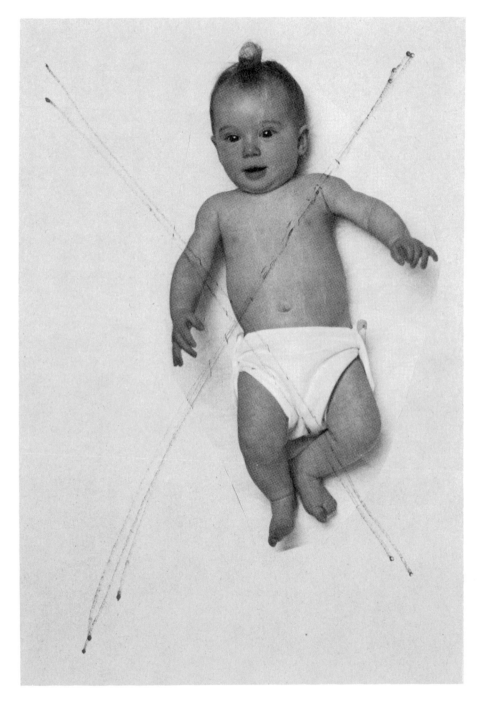

Figure 14

The treatment team initially found Ernest to be relatively compliant but available for only superficial relationships. Over five months the team members observed no significant change in either his behavior or his capacity for insight. Ernest appeared to benefit least of all the participants from the milieu approach, retaining his withdrawn, unexpressive presentation. His participation in art therapy paralleled his lack of progress within the milieu, although he did seem to benefit from the extended opportunity to record and concretely delineate his experiences over time.

Figures 15 and 16 are two pages from the journal on which Ernest worked in each art therapy session. The journal project had been initiated as an effort to provide the youngster with an ongoing vehicle for the development of self-expression. Although Ernest remained disconnected and tangential in his discussion of his selections each week, the process of a weekly addition to his "diary" appeared to provide him with a sense of continuity and self-identification. The imagery itself suggests both his infantile concerns and his struggles to develop autonomously despite major developmental disabilities. Ernest appeared trapped within rigid defensive structures and would likely remain compliantly responsive (in the milieu) and self-expressively limited (in psychotherapy).

Billy

Billy is a seventeen-year-old boy repeatedly diagnosed throughout his records as psychotic. Abandoned at birth by his parents, he was raised by adoptive parents against whom there are allegations of physical abuse.

In the initial art task (Figure 17), Billy selected images that suggest both his concerns with sexuality and his tendency to revert to a well-developed fantasy life to avoid threatening self-disclosure. His escapist imagery and his repeated inclusion of masks and covered heads depict his defensive posture and possibly relate to the delusional system in which he often lives.

The treatment team initially found Billy to be out of control behaviorally and unavailable for relationship. Over five months the team members consistently observed a worsening of his acting-out episodes and an increasing withdrawal into a delusional world as a way of avoiding intimacy. In his art therapy participation, Billy appeared to oscillate between increased self-expression and defensive retreat but never seemed to be able to integrate his temporary improvements.

209

holding the key to my
future right now

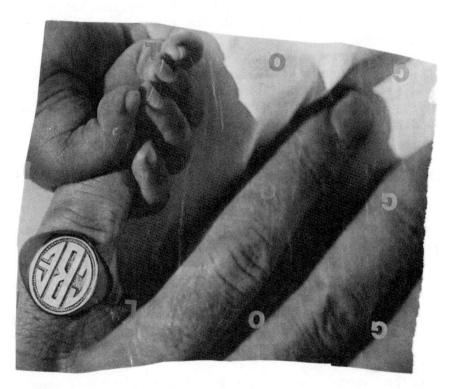

Figure 15

Figure 16

Figure 17

Figures 18 and 19, created in the same art therapy session, illustrate the manner in which Billy could be helped to let go of his delusional defenses if anxiety was at a minimum. After selecting the first picture and declaring that it looked "just like my family," Billy was encouraged to pick three separate pictures to depict more about each of the family members. In the second collage Billy presented a more realistic picture of the dysfunctional relationships in his family of origin, able to successfully utilize the structured task to help him around his original defensive production. Despite this apparently hopeful event (and many others like it), Billy was never able to sustain his expressive development and his delusional system remained an ever-present and ever-enlarging reality.

Figure 20, a drawing created spontaneously by Billy in an art therapy session, provides metaphorical access into the boy's defensive retreats. He described the picture in terms of the scuba diver who would rather explore the underwater than be with the people above. It appeared that Billy's avoidant interactions with the treatment team paralleled his fleeting retreats from whatever self-expression the art therapy modality was temporarily able to catalyze.

Violet

Violet is a twelve-year-old girl who experienced a series of placements since early childhood. Allegations of sexual abuse and mother's alternative lifestyle have contributed to her identity and developmental confusions.

Violet refused to participate in the initial art task, resisting both the art process and the treatment relationship offered. Although the youngster's resistance was calm and friendly, she was adamant in her decision to utilize the art materials only for a stereotypical crafts project she had learned in a previous placement. Her efforts to take control of this apparently threatening modality suggest the rigid defense mechanisms she utilizes to avoid expression and acknowledgment of her internal experiences.

The treatment team initially found Violet to be guardedly available for relationship and only moderately containable in her behavior. However, over five months observations changed dramatically. During the first three months Violet was observed to become calmer, less volatile and much closer to the treatment team members. Significantly, however, this improvement reversed itself over the last two months of observation

213

Figure 18

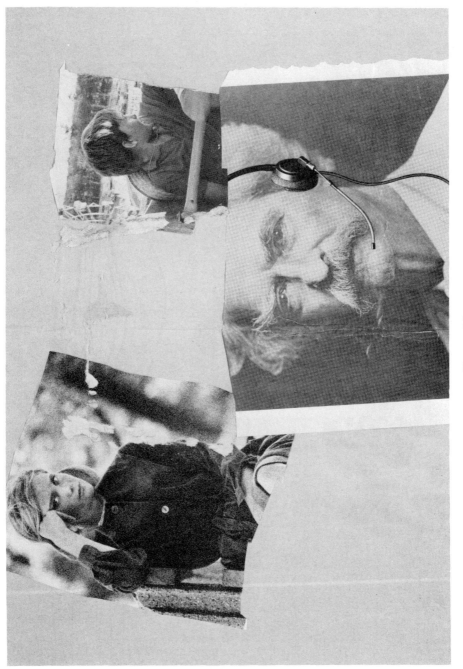

Figure 19

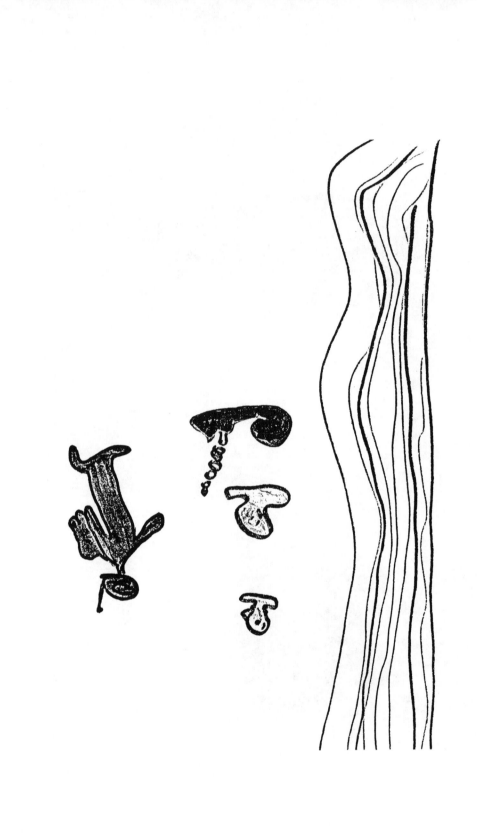

Figure 20

and Violet's behavior/provocativeness worsened. Although the team members were frustrated with this apparent regression, the girl's evolving participation in art therapy provides clues into the meaning of her milieu difficulties.

Violet's initial stereotypical involvement in the art process gradually relaxed. Despite her avoidant maneuvers to resist the development of a close therapeutic relationship, her evolving comfort in the art modality eased her defenses. Paralleling an increased investment within the milieu observed by the treatment team members, Violet began to allow the art process to become a self-expressive vehicle.

Figure 21 is typical of the very first drawings that Violet did in art therapy. Although the imagery suggests her defended posture (i.e., the elaborately colored windows blocking access to the home) and emotional limitations (the figure's lack of arms), the drawing depicts emerging self-expression. The content of the picture and the associated story (about a girl coming out of her backyard where she had been hiding and preparing for a trip to the market) suggest her increasing availability.

Just as this drawing indicates Violet's beginning utilization of the therapeutic opportunities in art expression, it also provides help in understanding the reasons for the youngster's retreat from the behavioral gains she had thus far achieved. Self-disclosure, intimacy and affective acknowledgment were experiences for which she had no preparation, and as consequences of emotional progress these achievements were overwhelming. Scared by the very successes so appreciatively observed by the treatment team, Violet regressed to a more familiar and less demanding mode of operation. Her final collage (Figure 22) attests to her improvement despite the treatment team's disappointing behavioral observations.

Violet selected the two pictures in Figure 22 in response to the therapist's request to choose images that depicted her current experiences. Although she insisted she had selected the pictures because she "just liked them," she seems to have used the collage to accurately portray her emotional reawakening and developmental efforts. Both the females portrayed have their faces turned away but the words and the movement within the imagery suggest reorienting activity. Art therapy seems to have provided Violet with the opportunity to share and record progress that she was as of yet incapable of demonstrating within the milieu. In this case example the self-expressive progress evidenced in the art

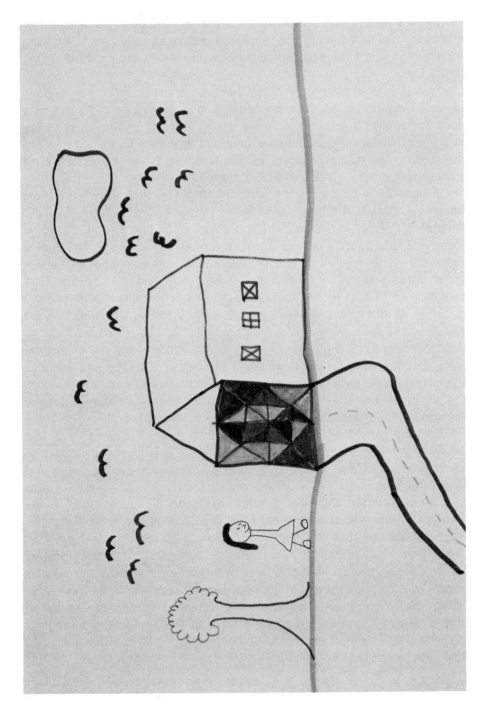

Figure 21

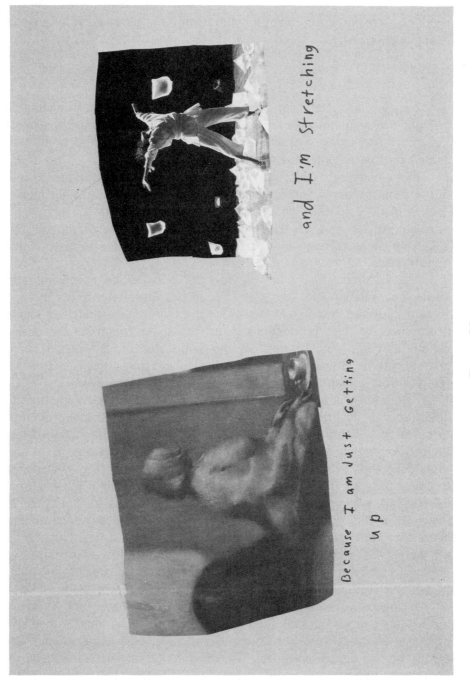

and I'm Stretching

Because I am Just Getting up

Figure 22

productions makes comprehensible the parallel but paradoxical behavioral changes observed.

Nancy

Nancy is a sixteen-year-old girl with limited intellectual functioning brought up in an impulse-ridden family. Sexual abuse charges against the father resulted in removal of all the children from the home and subsequent placement for Nancy.

In the initial art task (Figure 23), Nancy selected images that portray her infantile concerns and dependency needs on the left and her typical pattern of denying and "beautifying" her experiences on the right. Her poignant collage and her immediate acceptance of the therapeutic relationship suggest that this adolescent was eager for self-expressive opportunities.

The treatment team initially found Nancy to be compliant and available for relationship. Very little change was observed over five months (Figure 23a) and Nancy was generally perceived in the milieu as stable and responsive. Her productions in art therapy substantiate the observations that her defense mechanisms, supported by the milieu, were operating well. However, her artwork also indicates that a major depressive core remained unexposed and potentially explosive.

Figure 24 is characteristic of Nancy's drawings in which she heavily embellished a nevertheless empty-looking house in a symbolic attempt to cover up/beautify her damaged sense of self. Over the course of art therapy her repetitive drawings of this same house appeared more and more decorated but less and less inhabited. Occasionally Nancy was able to create artwork (Figure 25) that seemed to slip through her defensive hold, usually relying on collage pictures to stimulate otherwise unavailable material. In this drawing/collage, the destroyed, decaying construction belies that apparent facade of her more defended drawings. Apparently art therapy offered Nancy a nonthreatening opportunity to explore the material that she needed to defend against so rigidly in order to maintain herself in the milieu.

Despite the treatment team's sense that Nancy was not acknowledging her depression, her final collage (Figure 26) suggests that she had begun to recognize her boredom and rage, both external manifestations of her depressive core. The imagery of restless adolescents is remarkably different from the pretty and infantile picture in her first collage. This adolescent's tremendous improvement in self-expression substantiated the treatment team's observation of overall gains. Apparently as her security in the milieu increased so did her comfort with self-disclosure and the acknowledgment of feelings.

Charlene

Charlene is a fifteen-year-old girl with an extensive history of placements and aggressive behavior. Raised by a mother whose long-term involvement with drugs and alcohol resulted in her current incarceration, Charlene has little relationship with her emotionally unavailable father and presents as angry and "streetwise."

In the initial art task (Figure 27) Charlene was able to select directly self-representational images, but she requested that the therapist help structure the experience by writing down the dictated captions. Charlene's emotionally honest response to the therapist's request to outline the most important image (upper right) suggests her capacity to utilize the art process to directly explore her affective experiences. The caption reads "This is me but it reminds me of my mom because she doesn't have a home."

The treatment team initially found Charlene to be disruptive in her behavior and only intermittently available for relationship. Over five months the treatment team members observed both her behavior problems and her accessibility for intimacy increasing substantially. This seemingly contradictory development can be explained as her artwork from the same period is examined.

Always eager to participate in art therapy sessions, Charlene's involvement in the art process was spontaneous and undefended. Figure 28 illustrates the manner in which she often completed images that had begun with doodles or scribbles. Charlene described this figure as "pink and soft on the inside but nasty and bristling on the outside." Able to tolerate the therapist's reflections about the similarities between the girl (so tightly contained with anxiously drawn lines) and her own explosive behavior, Charlene seemed capable of utilizing self-expression for self-understanding.

Figure 29, a spontaneous marker drawing, is characteristic of a long series of productions in which Charlene utilized the art process to explore her concerns with containment and impulsive explosions. This example was created in reaction to a particularly stressful episode in the

221

Figure 23

222

Figure 23a

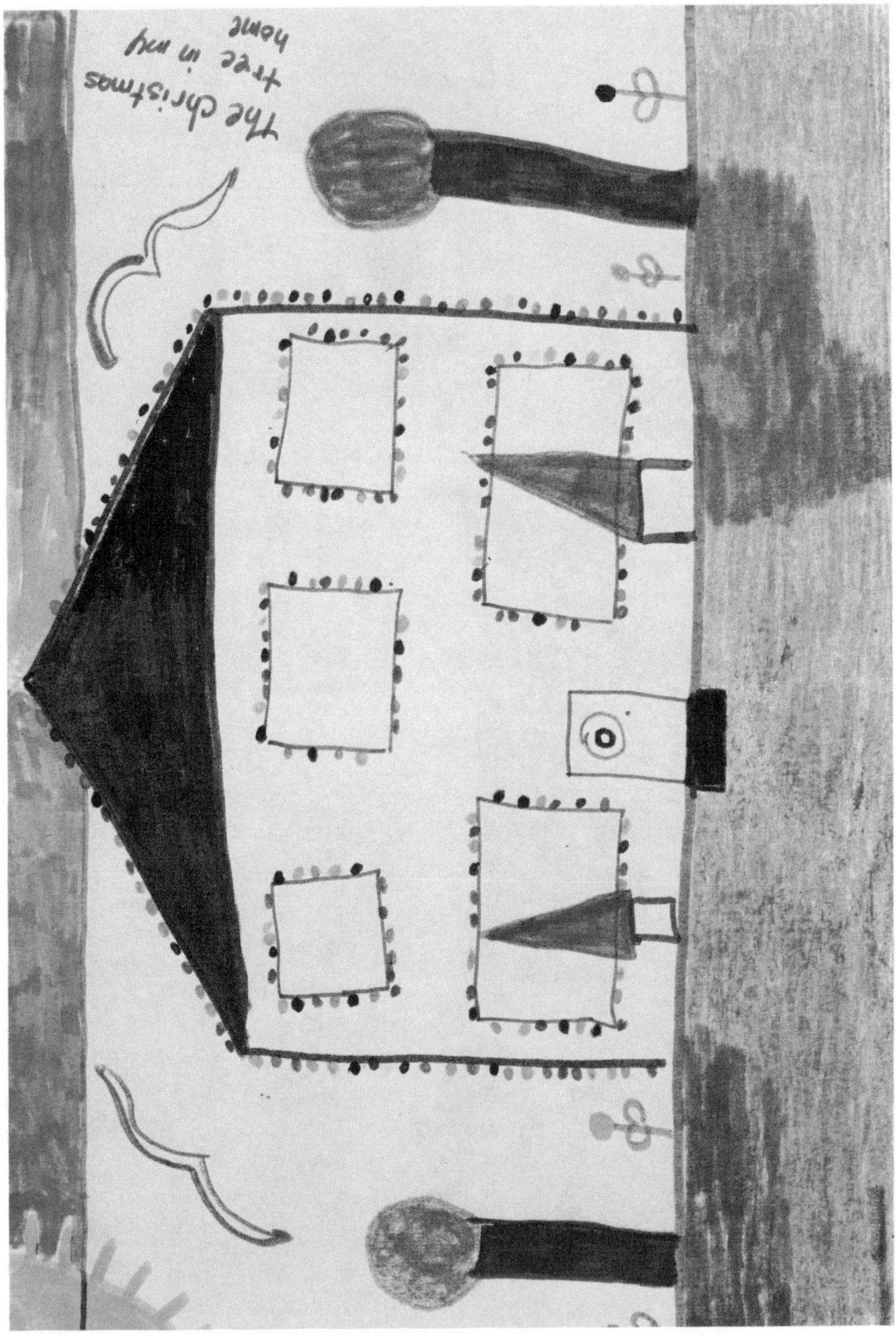

Figure 24

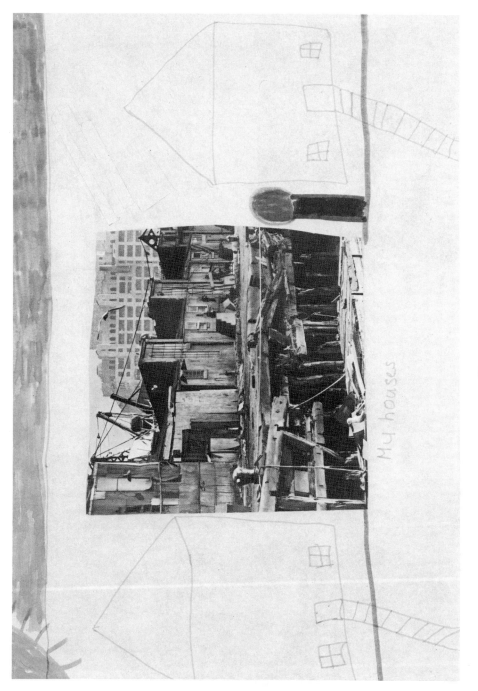

My houses

Figure 25

The big story

Figure 26

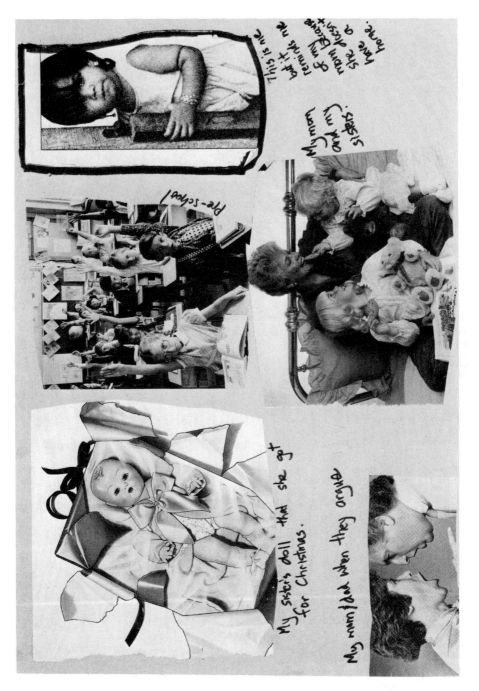

Figure 27

227

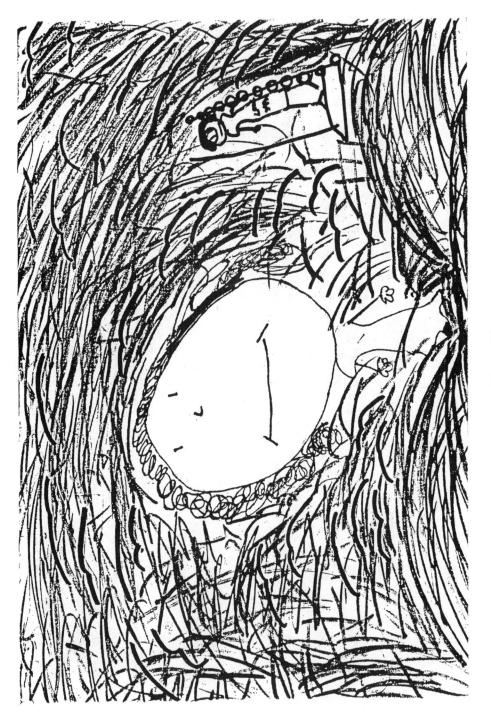

Figure 28

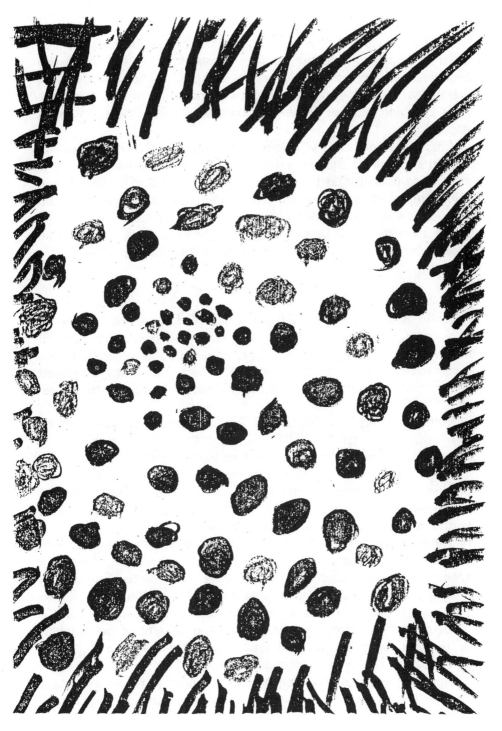

Figure 29

classroom and helped her understand the crucial relationships between internal feelings and external behavior. Over time, as her expressive productions became increasingly self-disclosing, Charlene became more vulnerable, a factor that likely contributed significantly to both her more volatile behavior and her closer relationships with the treatment team members.

Charlene's final collage (Figure 30) speaks powerfully about her increased capacity to share her feelings and internal experiences. It is significant to note that in this production, a powerful expression about her long repressed anger toward her mother, she no longer relied on the therapist's help to caption her selections. In this case example, the evolving art productions provide help in understanding the intrapsychic process behind the adolescent's parallel behavioral deterioration.

Janise

Janise is a thirteen-year-old girl with a history of multiple foster and group home failures because of violent outbursts. After removal from her mother at birth, Janise was placed in an adoptive family where she suffered from neglect and cruelty. At intake Janise was diagnosed by the consulting psychiatrist as schizophrenic and mildly mentally retarded.

In the initial art task (Figure 31), Janise created a poignant expression of sadness and family conflict. Although the pictures speak clearly about the adolescent's depression and concerns, Janise was unable to discuss the imagery and she denied its potential relationship to her own experiences. The affective quality of this collage and the girl's inability to recognize its self-representational function suggest her characteristic defensive reaction against the acknowledgment of feelings.

The treatment team initially found Janise to have very limited control over her behavior and to be unavailable for relationship. Very little change (if any) was observed in Janise over five months. Similarly in art therapy, Janise appeared unable to move past her limited ability to impulsively express internal turmoil. With no apparent skills to contain or understand her expression, the themes and content of her artwork were powerful but repetitive and unchanging. Figures 32 and 33 are characteristic of her self-representative imagery.

Figure 32 portrays a one-legged horse, unable to mobilize a return to its family and sadly expressing hopelessness. Similarly, Figure 33 presents a story about a mother who, because of the Walkman radio carefully drawn into the picture, is unable to hear her children crying. The unavailable mother and the powerless child, both aspects of Janise's internal experiences, are expressed symbolically. Throughout the five months of observation, Janise's artwork continued to explode with affect. Similarly her behavior suggested her limited ability to contain or understand her internal process. Art therapy appears to have done little more than monitor her problematic participation within the milieu. Just as explosiveness and unpredictability characterized her behavior within the milieu, this adolescent's art productions reflected the same kind of impulsiveness.

CONCLUSIONS

Defensive Quality of Initial Artwork

It is worthwhile to note the similarities in the artwork of the adolescents participating in this program. Because of the severity of their histories and disturbances and because of the adolescent dynamic of overreactive defense mechanisms, the initial collages reflect little invest-ment in the art process and an overall indifference to the self-expressive process. Hastily selected pictures, randomly placed and inadequately glued to the paper, suggest the youngsters' low self-esteem as manifested in their perceptions of their own efforts being "worthless." The collages of all ten adolescents in the program, although depicting to varying degrees internal conflicts and feelings, more powerfully illustrate the defensive structure the youngsters utilize to fight against the recognition of internal experiences. It is for this reason that unconsciously motivated behavioral outbursts characterized the functioning of these girls and boys. Just as the art productions reflected constructed efforts to repress/avoid/deny/diffuse/project/displace and/or otherwise resist feelings, the behav-ioral difficulties described by the milieu staff represented maladaptive outbursts of these poorly contained feelings. Violet is a particularly good example of an adolescent whose rigid defense mechanisms (demonstrated in her unwillingness to participate in unfamiliar art tasks) led to explosive outbursts in which her behavior provided an outlet for the inefficiently contained affect. Johnny, on the other hand, represents a different kind of adolescent defensive process. Less sophisticated than Violet, both his behavioral outbursts and his early art productions reflected his inability

231

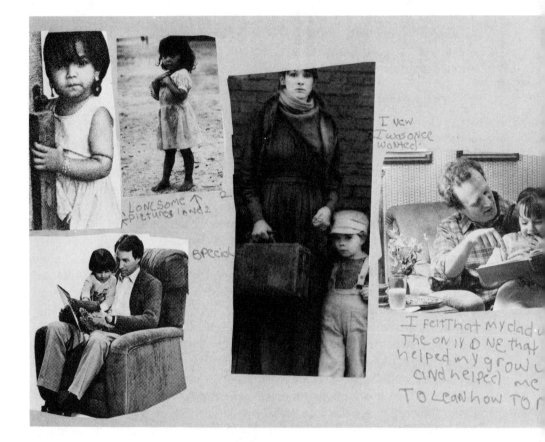

Figure 30

232

so HELPED ME BY
WAlKiNG
ME to schOOL

This is wheN I WAS
JUST BORN my my moM
did Not help me grow up
my father did and I Love him

true.
And its
mom.
my
than
more

233

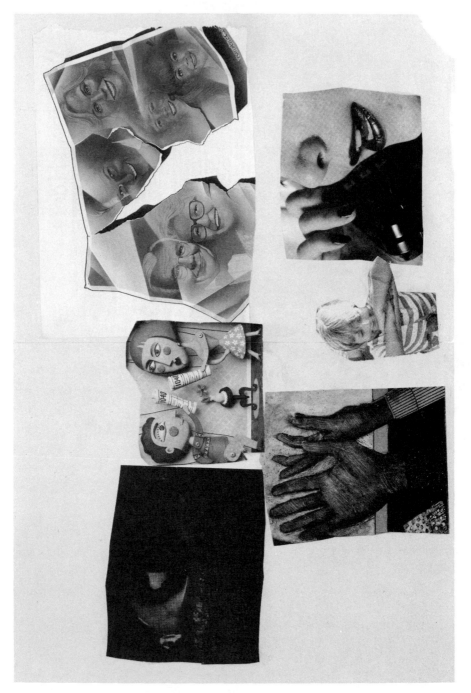

Figure 31

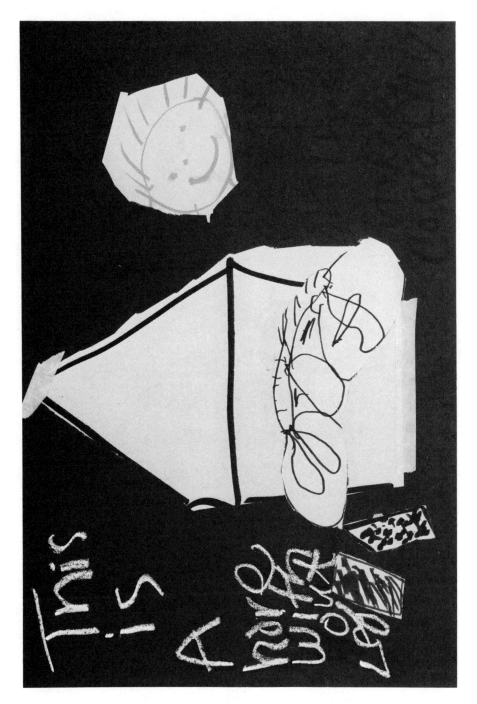

Figure 32

235

Figure 33

to contain his impulses/confusion and his overwhelmed response to the flooding overstimulation caused by his feelings. All the youngsters appeared trapped by their self-expressive limitations and to some degree victims of the behavioral consequences.

Response to Treatment and Development of Relationship

For all of the adolescents involved in treatment art therapy provided a vehicle for the development of a nonthreatening relationship. The art process allowed the youngsters to retain control of the evolving intimacy by regulating the degree to which they utilized the self-expressive potential. Consequently, even the most severely disturbed of the participants were able to benefit from the structured approach to self-disclosure offered in this modality. Three of the youngsters clearly exemplify this limited but important response to the art therapy approach. Jim's use of the collage process to discharge and project his internal obsessions with violent sexuality illustrates the manner in which this modality can offer undirected opportunities to alleviate turbulent material. As Jim felt increasingly comfortable within the therapeutic relationship, he was able to use the release valve that the collage process had become to him. Uninterpreted, unresolved, the images simply delineate a process of discharge that helped the boy contain himself and progress (however minimally) within the milieu. In a similar manner, Ernest's response to the art therapy approach illustrates the relationship aspect of treatment. This boy's journal, itself a symbol for the containing continuance of the therapist's presence, offered an opportunity for sustained self-expression. Although Ernest appeared to make little progress in treatment, art therapy and the journal he created helped him gain a sense of who he was, over time and in contact with another person. Billy also provides an example of a disturbed adolescent's ability to benefit from art therapy (and the relationship provided) despite the lack of genuine progress in his self-expressive ability. Although Billy's delusional systems remained intact throughout treatment and continued to provide him with defensive retreats from the milieu, art therapy provided him with a vehicle to at least metaphorically express the material underlying his contrived fantasies. Billy was unable to decrease his defensive needs and progress in the day treatment program, but the imagery he created in art therapy provided the treatment team with an understanding of how damaged he felt.

237

Shifts/Evolution of Defense Mechanism

Other adolescents in this program responded more overtly to the potential of art therapy to augment self-expression. Two adolescents are discussed as examples of youngsters whose defensive structures were affected by their self-expression although neither was able to benefit immediately from the impact. Brian's need to defend completely against the art therapist and her self-expressive encouragement illustrates a very primitive shift in defenses. Frightened and overwhelmed by the release of affect catalyzed in the art process, Brian denied, undid, and diffused the experience. The process of projective identification allowed Brian to project his unacceptable feelings onto the art therapist and thereby rationalize his hostile resistance to continuing in the relationship. Although art therapy had helped Brian confront his defense mechanisms, he had been unable to tolerate this confrontation and had bolted from the process. It is hoped that future interactions would provide him with the opportunity to alter or even understand this process.

Nancy also exemplifies the adolescent process of shifting or evolving defense mechanisms in response to psychotherapeutic intervention. Like Brian she was able to demonstrate behavioral progress or at least behavioral maintenance in spite of massive therapeutic resistances. Rather than reacting against the process as Brian had, Nancy continued to participate in the process; she was adaptively able to utilize it for the defensive bolstering Brian had manifested in rejection. Nancy's increasingly defensive art productions suggested her current need to avoid psychotherapeutic progress in order to sustain her progress in the milieu. Despite (or perhaps because of) this bolstered resistance, Nancy was occasionally able to produce artwork that hinted at the feelings underlying her defenses. Art therapy had provided both adolescents with an opportunity that was rejected or resisted. As such it benefited the treatment team's understanding and allowed the adolescents to experience treatment options.

Development of Self-Expression

One adolescent is discussed as an example of the way that art therapy can function optimally. Not simply providing a vehicle for relationship (as with Jim, Ernest and Billy) or affecting the adolescent defensive structure (as with Brian and Nancy), it can also facilitate the development of self-expression subsequent to the relaxation of defenses. Charlene's increased capacity to directly explore her feelings in the art process illustrates this phenomenon. Able to utilize the art process for expression, exploration and ventilation, she consequently experienced increased exposure that did not prove to be too overwhelming. Charlene was able to expand upon her productions and develop self-awareness as she confronted her imagery. For this girl, and perhaps this girl alone, the art therapy process had proved itself to be truly psychotherapeutic.

SUMMARY

This clinical study has attempted to illustrate through case material the manner in which art therapy productions can be correlated with the treatment team's observations of adolescents participating in intensive milieu treatment. The developed correlations can enrich the clinical understanding of the therapeutic process as uniquely experienced by each of the youngsters. Each of the ten participating adolescents exhibited a very different reaction to the art therapy process. When understood as a parallel phenomenon to the behavioral changes observed in the milieu, the youngsters' self-expressive process becomes an invaluable assessment tool. With adolescents as severely disturbed as those participating in this program, no one treatment approach can be successful. Art therapy can help to provide concrete evidence that can be utilized to make sense of the often paradoxical and always complicated responses the youngsters are having to treatment.

References

American Psychiatric Association. *Diagnostic and Statistical Manual of Mental Disorders, Third Edition, Revised.* Washington, D.C.: APA, 1987.

Berkovitz, I. *Adolescents Grow in Groups.* New York: Brunner/Mazel, 1972.

Bettelheim, B., de Vryer, P., Mann, J., Norton, A., Noshpitz, J., & Pittenger, R. Psychotherapy and Residential Treatment. In American Association for Children's Residential Centers (Ed.), *From Chaos to Order: A Collective View of the Residential Treatment of Children.* New York: Child Welfare League of America, 1972.

Blos, P. *On Adolescence.* New York: Free Press, 1962.

Erikson, E. *Childhood and Society.* New York: W.W. Norton & Co., 1950.

Esman, A. *The Psychiatric Treatment of Adolescents.* New York: International Universities Press, 1983.

Evangelakis, M. *A Manual for Residential and Day Treatment of Children.* Springfield, IL: Charles C Thomas, 1974.

Josselyn, I. *Adolescence.* New York: Harper and Row, 1971.

Kramer, E. *Art Therapy in a Children's Community.* Springfield, IL: Charles C Thomas, 1958.

Landgarten, H. *Clinical Art Therapy.* New York: Brunner/Mazel, 1981.

Laufer, M., & Laufer, E. *Adolescence and Developmental Breakdown.* New Haven: Yale University Press, 1984.

Malmquist, C. *Handbook of Adolescence.* New York: Jason Aronson, 1978.

Mayer, M. The Parental Figures in Residential Treatment. *Social Service Review, 34,* 273–285, 1960.

Mirkin, M., & Koman, S. *Handbook of Adolescents and Family Therapy.* New York: Gardner Press, 1985.

Wadeson, H. *Art Psychotherapy.* New York: John Wiley & Sons, 1980.

Wolf, J., Willmuth, M., Gazda, T., & Watkins, A. The Role of Art in the Therapy of Anorexia Nervosa. *International Journal of Eating Disorders, 4(2),* 1985, 185–200.

Yalom, I. *The Theory and Practice of Group Psychotherapy.* New York: Basic Books, 1975.

Index

Defense mechanisms *(continued)*
  noncompromise, 11, 20
  regression, 10, 15
  repression, 11, 18
  reversal of affect, 10
Delinquency, 25, 26
Denial, as a defense, 11, 18
Developmental stage. *See* Adolescence
Diagnosis, 25
Diagnostic and Statistical Manual of
    Mental Disorders III-R, x, 9, 25–44
Directives, 18, 47, 52, 58–64, 114
Displacement, as a defense, 10
Disruptive Behavior Disorders, 25–34

Eating Disorders. *See* Anorexia Nervosa
Ego, 10
Empathy, 58
Erikson, E., 4
Esman, A., 46
Evangelekis, M., 117
Expression, 25
  acceptance of, 50
  distortions in, 114
  facilitation of, 50, 83, 238
  importance of, 5, 7, 183, 238

Family Art Therapy, 165
  case study, 166–182
Feelings, defenses against, 80, 119, 238
Felt markers, 52
Free expression, 50

Group Art Therapy, 133–164
  advantages of, 134
  case study, 135–164
  structuring, 136, 142
  termination of, 161
  transference in, 144

Identification, 4
Identity, 10
  conflicts, 5
  Disorder, 39–41
  search for, 4, 41
  sexual, 5
Impulses, 10, 11
Impulse control, 26
Individuation. *See* Separation
Insight. *See* Interpretation
Intact family. *See* Family Art Therapy
Intellectualization, as a defense, 11, 20
Interpretation, 54–55, 114
Interventions, of the art therapist:
  facilitating, 50–53
  interpreting, 54–55

structuring, 52
Intimacy, 122
Isolation, as a defense, 11, 22

Josselyn, I., 134
Journals, 6, 65–68

Kramer, E., 117

Landgarten, H., 6, 135
Latency stage of development, 5

Malmquist, C., 5, 10, 25–41
Mayer, M., 116
Media, 68–77
Metaphors, 55, 64, 120. *See also*
    Interpretation
Milieu treatment, xi, 115–131

Narcissism, as a defense, 10, 15
Noncompromise, as a defense, 11, 20
Norton, A., 118
Noshpitz, J., 118

Oppositional Defiant Disorder, 30
Overanxious Disorder, 39

Paints, 74
Pencil, 72
Pittenger, R., 118
Psychosis, 98, 114
Puberty, 4

Regression:
  as a defense, 10, 15
  in the service of the ego, 76–77
Residential treatment, 115–131
Repression, as a defense, 11, 18
Resistance, 59, 89, 231
Reversal of affect, as a defense, 10
Review of art productions, 64–65

Scapegoating, 148
Schizophrenia, 98
Schulman, I., 146
Sculptures, 81
Self-expression. *See* Expression
Self-image, 30, 106
Separation:
  task of, 4, 10
  conflicts over, 61
Separation Anxiety Disorder, 34–39
Sexuality, 5
Symbols:
  augmentation of, 50
  of self, 86, 92, 98

244